THE

Cars and Trucks
Puzzle and Activity Book

Race your way through miles of turbo-charged fun!

Charles Timmerman, Founder of Funster.com

Adams Media
Avon, Massachusetts

EDITORIAL
Publishing Director: Gary M. Krebs
Associate Managing Editor: Laura M. Daly
Associate Copy Chief: Brett Palana-Shanahan
Acquisitions Editor: Kate Burgo
Associate Production Editor: Casey Ebert

PRODUCTION
Production Director: Susan Beale
Production Manager: Michelle Roy Kelly
Series Designers: Colleen Cunningham, Erin Ring
Layout and Graphics: Brewster Brownville,
   Colleen Cunningham, Jennifer Oliveira
Cover Layout: Paul Beatrice, Matt LeBlanc, Erick
   DaCosta

An Everything® Series Book.
Everything® and everything.com® are registered trademarks of F+W Publications, Inc.

Published by Adams Media, an F+W Publications Company
57 Littlefield Street, Avon, MA 02322. U.S.A.
www.adamsmedia.com

ISBN 10: 1-59337-703-7
ISBN 13: 978-1-59337-703-8

Printed in the United States of America.

J I H G F E D C B A

This publication is designed to provide accurate and authoritative information with regard to the subject
matter covered. It is sold with the understanding that the publisher is not engaged in rendering legal,
accounting, or other professional advice. If legal advice or other expert assistance is required, the ser-
vices of a competent professional person should be sought.
> —From a *Declaration of Principles* jointly adopted by a Committee of the
> American Bar Association and a Committee of Publishers and Associations

Many of the designations used by manufacturers and sellers to distinguish their products are claimed as
trademarks. When those designations appear in this book and Adams Media was aware of a trademark
claim, the designations have been printed with initial capital letters.

Cover illustrations by Dana Regan.
Interior illustrations and puzzles by Charles Timmerman.
Chapter opener art by Kurt Dolber.

This book is available at quantity discounts for bulk purchases.
For information, please call 1-800-872-5627.

See the entire Everything® series at *www.everything.com*.

Contents

Introduction / v

Chapter 1: Racecars / 1

Chapter 2: Trucks That Haul / 13

Chapter 3: The Horseless Carriage / 25

Chapter 4: Engines / 37

Chapter 5: Road Trip / 49

Chapter 6: Emergency! / 61

Chapter 7: Service Stations / 73

Chapter 8: Construction Vehicles / 85

Chapter 9: The Ice Cream Truck / 97

Appendix: Fun Web Sites and Games to Play in the Car / 109

Puzzle Answers / 110

Dedicated to Barek and Asher.

Introduction

This book comes fully loaded with fun! Get ready to turbocharge your brain as you rip through these pages. Every vehicle from super-fast sports cars to radical trucks is covered as you puzzle your way around the roadways and race tracks in this book. All of the nitty-gritty details down to the nuts and bolts will appear in puzzles about engines, service stations, and horseless carriages. It's all topped off with a visit to the ice cream truck for some puzzling treats.

Just about every kind of puzzle and game imaginable is found under the hood. The tank is filled with plenty of word games to keep you moving down the highway: crosswords, word searches, rhyming games, and others. Shift into high gear with amusing math and logic puzzles. Entertaining picture puzzles like mazes and hidden pictures will keep you speeding through these pages.

Fun is the destination of this book! But your parents will be happy to know that your brain will be getting a healthy mental workout. And you can probably find a puzzle or two that will amuse, and maybe even stump, Mom or Dad.

So start your engines and put the pedal to the metal. Just be sure to keep your hands on the wheel and your eyes on the road as you begin this wild ride through puzzling fun!

Find the Pictures

Can you find each of these pictures on another page of this book? There is one picture from each chapter. Write the chapter number in the space below each picture.

Chapter 1

Racecars

Stopwatch Mysteries

These stopwatches were used to measure how long it took racecars to go around a track. Can you figure out the times on the fourth stopwatches? Hint: look for a pattern in the first three stopwatches.

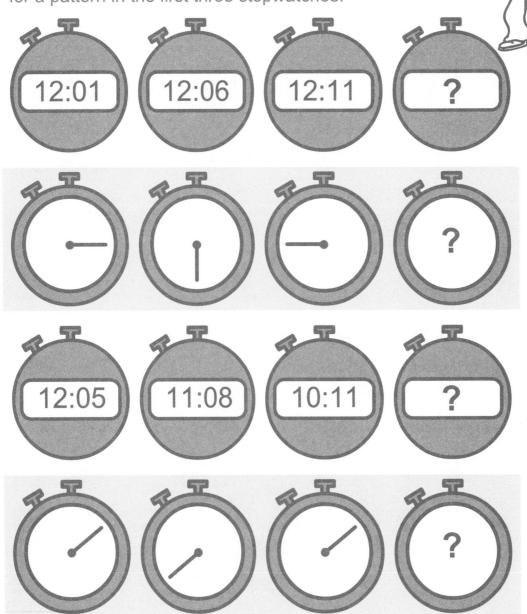

Crazy Driver

Pick the correct set of turns that will steer the car around the course.
L=Left Turn   R=Right Turn

A: L,R,L,R,L,R,R,L,L,L,R,L   C: L,R,L,L,L,R,R,L,L,L,R,L

B: L,R,L,L,L,R,R,R,L,L,R,L   D: L,R,L,L,L,R,R,L,L,R,L

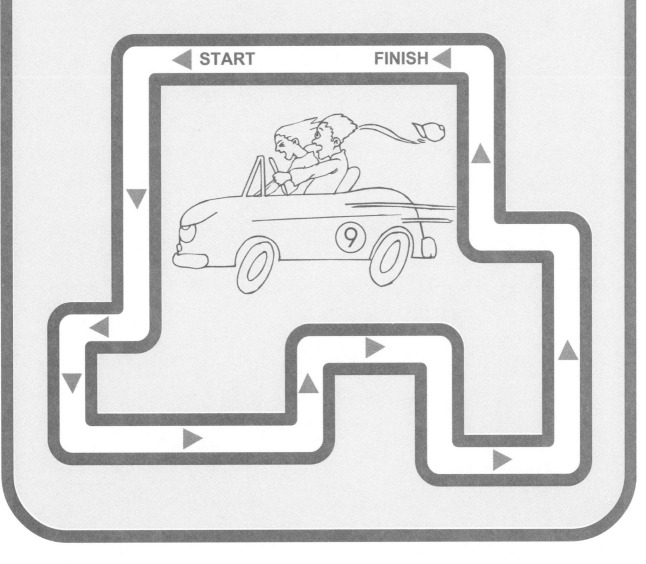

Fast Cars

There are at least 10 differences in these two collections of fast cars. How many can you find?

Fruit Race

Which racecar will score the most points? Each car will pick up all of the fruit in its lane. Use this key to determine the points awarded:

=3   =1

=7   =4

Fuel Man

Can you help fuel man deliver gas and oil to the racecars? To be fair, each racecar needs to be given the exact same quantity.

The numbers on these gas cans tell how many gallons of gas each contains. Use a single straight line to divide the gas into two equal amounts.

The numbers on these oil cans tell how many quarts of oil each contains. Use a single straight line to divide the oil into two equal amounts.

Math Races

The last digits will be the year of the first Daytona 500:

2	9	3	8
+1	-7	+6	-5
+4	-1	-8	+6
-5	+4	+3	-9
+6	-2	+5	+4
-7	+6	-4	+5

Add up all of the numbers to find out how many times Richard Petty has won the Daytona 500:

+5   -2
   +6   +3
-9   +1
+6   -8
-4   +9
   -5   -4
+7   +2

Race to the Checkered Flag

Travel from START to FINISH by moving up, down, left, or right. For each move, the flag should have one more square filled in.

START

FINISH

Racing Code

Each picture stands for one of two letters.

For example, 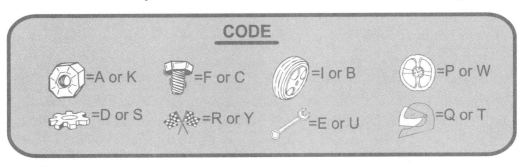 sometimes stands for an E and other times for a U.

Can you find five words that describe a winning racecar?

CODE

= A or K   = F or C   = I or B   = P or W

= D or S   = R or Y   = E or U   = Q or T

1. ____ ____ ____ ____
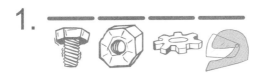

2. ____ ____ ____ ____ ____ ____
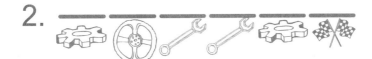

3. ____ ____ ____ ____ ____
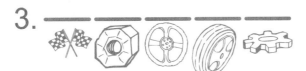

4. ____ ____ ____ ____ ____

5. ____ ____ ____ ____ ____

Racing Rhymes

Use these pictures to figure out words that rhyme with *race*.
When you are done, say the words in order really fast for fun.

_ _ _ _   _ _ _ _ _   _ _ _

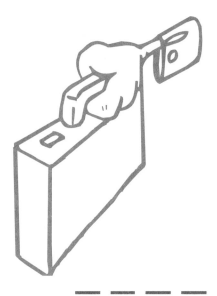 

_ _ _ _ _   _ _ _ _

Start Your Engines

Color in all of the boxes that look like this: /

You will find out what is sometimes called "the greatest spectacle in racing."

An aMAZEing Race

Monster's Truck

Monster has been reading in the library and needs help finding his truck. Can you find Monster's truck using these clues?

1. Monster's truck does not have a heart above it.
2. Monster's truck is not in the first column.
3. Monster's truck does not have a cat below it.
4. Monster's truck is not in a row with a fish and a turtle.

Numbers Convoy

Trucks often travel together in groups known as convoys. The convoys on this page all have a pattern to the numbers on their trucks. Can you determine the last number in each convoy?

Special Delivery

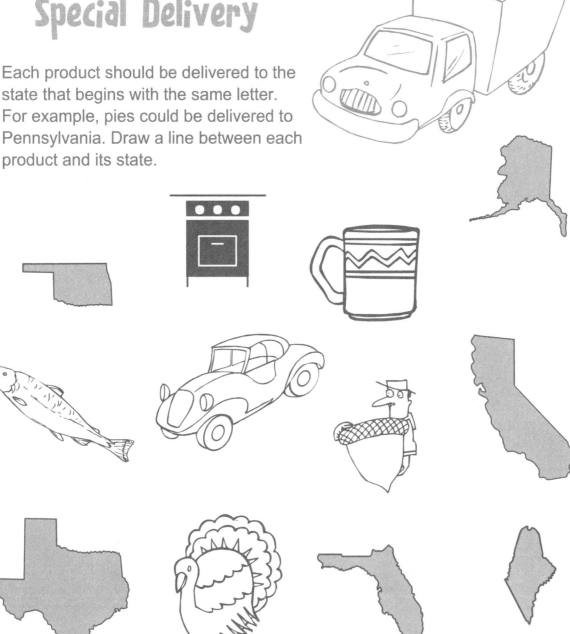

Each product should be delivered to the state that begins with the same letter. For example, pies could be delivered to Pennsylvania. Draw a line between each product and its state.

Twisty Routes

Find a route to get from the factory to the store and a route to get from the farm to the store. These routes might overlap.

STORE

Circle Movers

Circle the truck carrying the most circles.

Postman

The U.S. Postal Service delivers about 100 million First-Class letters every day. Can you tell which of these letters is the one that should be delivered? It has all the following characteristics:

- Three hearts
- Smiley face stamp
- Three triangles at bottom
- To: Jill

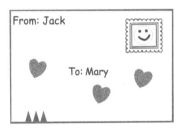

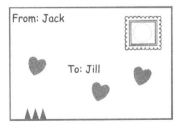

Wear and Tear

These trucks have logged a lot of hard miles. The city they came from was originally painted on their side, but the letters have partially worn off. Can you figure out what city each truck is from? Hint: they are all U.S. state capitals.

Flying Wheels

What has four wheels and flies?

To discover the answer to the riddle, follow these instructions:

1. Cross out the Rs and Es in row 1.
2. Cross out the Ys and Cs in row 2.
3. Cross out the As and Bs in row 3.
4. Cross out the Zs and Ds in row 4.

1: EAGERRAE

2: YRYBCCAG

3: BBBEATAR

4: ZZUDCZDK

Answer:_____

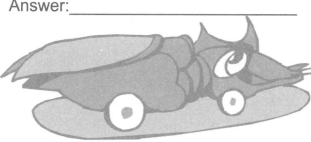

Scrambled Groceries

These trucks all deliver food to grocery stores. For some reason the letters on the trucks are scrambled. Can you figure out what each truck is delivering?

_____

_____

_____

_____

10-4 Good Buddy!

Truck drivers talk to each other using CB radios. They use 10-codes to transmit messages quickly. For example, 10-4 means "OK, message received." Translate the message below using this substitution code: 1=A, 2=B, 3=C, etc.

Q. $\overline{23}$ $\overline{8}$ $\overline{1}$ $\overline{20}$ $\overline{9}$ $\overline{19}$ $\overline{2}$ $\overline{9}$ $\overline{7}$,

$\overline{23}$ $\overline{8}$ $\overline{9}$ $\overline{20}$ $\overline{5}$, $\overline{7}$ $\overline{9}$ $\overline{22}$ $\overline{5}$ $\overline{19}$

$\overline{13}$ $\overline{9}$ $\overline{12}$ $\overline{11}$, $\overline{1}$ $\overline{14}$ $\overline{4}$ $\overline{8}$ $\overline{1}$ $\overline{19}$

$\overline{15}$ $\overline{14}$ $\overline{5}$ $\overline{8}$ $\overline{15}$ $\overline{18}$ $\overline{14}$?

A. $\overline{1}$ $\overline{13}$ $\overline{9}$ $\overline{12}$ $\overline{11}$ $\overline{20}$ $\overline{18}$ $\overline{21}$ $\overline{3}$ $\overline{11}$.

23

What's Missing?

Which letter is missing from the mixed-up alphabet on each truck?
The four missing letters will spell a type of truck.

Chapter 3

The Horseless Carriage

Horseless Pioneers

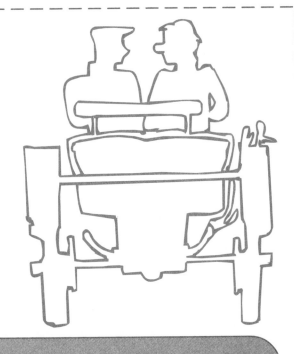

The first horseless carriage in America was produced in 1893 by brothers Charles and Frank Duryea. The puzzle below will reveal who is credited with making the automobile popular.

Carefully follow these instructions with the grid of letters to the right.

1. Cross out any As.

2. Cross out any Js.

3. Cross out any double letters (like DD).

4. Cross out any Ys in the third row.

5. Cross out all letters in the second column.

JXHBBJEA

NLRYAFJO

ALYCCRYD

Wheels Turning

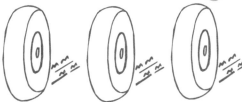

Multiple Choice: Approximately how old is the oldest wheel ever found by archaeologists?
(A) 1 million years old
(B) 50,000 years old
(C) 5,000 years old
(D) 500 years old

Glove Compartment

In the early days of the automobile it was common to wear gloves while driving. So the glove compartment was actually used to store gloves. Today we still have glove compartments, but they are rarely used to store gloves!

Can you find the two gloves that match on this page?

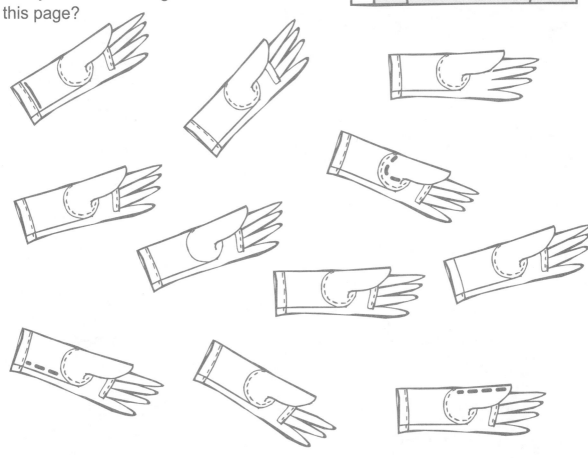

A Horse of Course

In the early 1900s, horses were replaced by automobiles as a primary form of transportation. Would you like to ride a horse to school or the store? Use the letters in **HORSE** to find words for the pictures below.

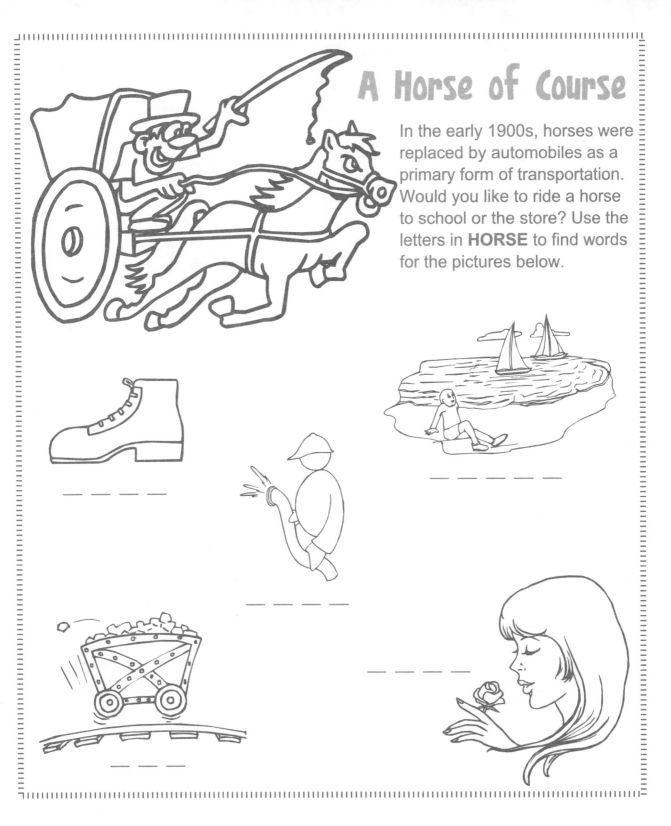

_ _ _ _

_ _ _ _

_ _ _ _

_ _ _ _

_ _ _ _

Striped Automobiles

"You can have any color as long as it is black," boasted Henry Ford about his early cars. "We want stripes!," demands the tiger family.

Match these four patterns to the samples below.

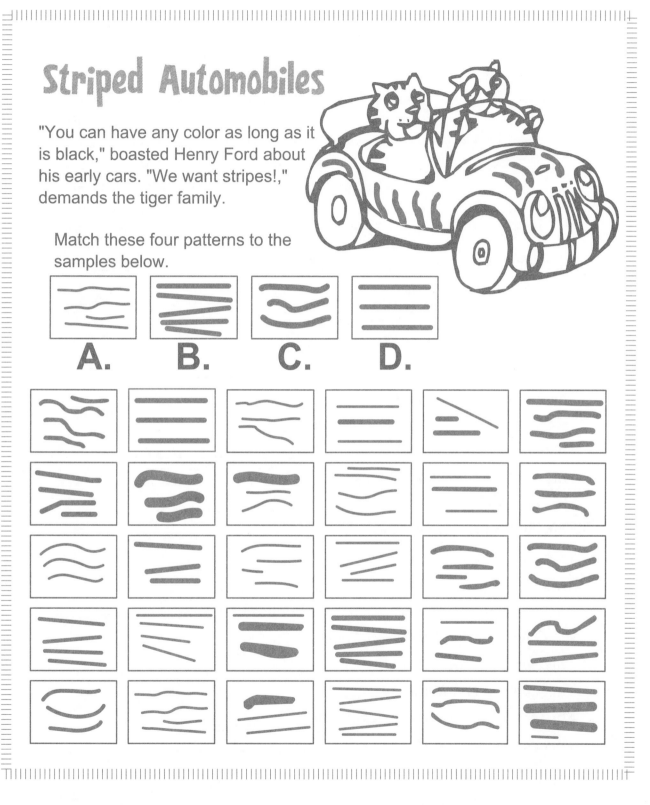

A.   B.   C.   D.

Model T for Tiger

The Ford Motor Company made over 15 million Model Ts from 1908 through 1927. It is one of the most successful automobiles of all time. Not as popular were Ford Models A, B, C, and so on up to T. Can you give each car model a name of an animal that starts with the same letter? All of the animals (except for one) appear on the next page.

This car has a toothy grill: Model A_____

This car is huggable: Model B_____

This car has a hump: Model C_____

This car waddles: Model D_____

This car has a long trunk: Model E_____

This car can swim: Model F_____

This car is for tall people: Model G_____

This car is enormous: Model H_____

This car has scaly upholstery: Model I_____

This car is very fast: Model J_____

This car really jumps: Model K_____

This car can roar: Model L_____

This car can swing: Model M_____

This car could be called Salamander: Model N_____

WHO would want this car?: Model O_____

This car can talk: Model P_____

This car can fly: Model Q_____

This car helps Santa deliver: Model R_____

This car is very slow: Model S_____

Can you find all of the animals for Models A to S on this page? Uh oh! Which one of the animals has wandered away?

Famous Inventors

The invention of the automobile changed society. Can you match each invention below with the name of a person associated with it?

Telegraph

Benjamin Franklin

Orville Wright

George Eastman

Bifocals

Thomas Edison

Samuel Morse

If you invented a car, what name would you give it? Circle the car names that are names of people who built automobiles:

Volkswagon

Ford

Roadster

General Motors

Mercedes-Benz

Chrysler

Porsche

Batmobile

Acme

Oldsmobile

Jones

Chevrolet

Wheels Go Round

Early cars had wheels that looked similar to bicycle tires. They had spokes made of wood! Can you find your way through this wheel maze?

START

FINISH

Rearrange these jumbled letters to find out what people turned to start the original horseless carriages. (Hint: it wasn't a key!)

AMPLEX
ARNOLT
BANTAM
BLOMSTROM
BRISTOL
CALVERT
CAMERON
CROSLEY
DINGFELDER
DUESENBERG
ELGIN
ESSEX
EXCALIBUR
FALCON
FLANDERS
GOODSPEED
HALLADAY
HUDSON
KAISER
KIDDER
LOCOMOBILE
MARQUETTE
MAXWELL
NASH
OVERLAND
PACKARD
PEERLESS
PRATT
SENECA
STUYVESANT
TUCKER
WINDSOR
ZIMMERMAN

Early Car Biz

In the early days of the automobile industry there were hundreds of car companies. Many of these companies closed or were bought by other companies.

Find the names of the early car companies in the list to the left by looking up, down, across, backward, and diagonally in the letters below. Some letters may appear in more than one word.

```
R X K I D D E R A C E N E S F
E X E S S E L R E E P O Z D A
S M R L O T S I R B M S I R L
I D O E P L U H O C K D M A C
A L N R D M A Y A D E U M K O
K Z L A T L A M V U H E C N
B A Z E L S E T T E U Q R A M
E F Z A W R M F R S S I M P R
Y L D L O X E O G E O A A R O
M A T N A B A V L N V K N A S
Y N L L O C O M O B I L E T D
V D I G O O D S P E E D A T N
X E X C A L I B U R L X V C I
C R O S L E Y E L G I N P Z W
H S A N A R N O L T U C K E R
```

Assembly Line

Henry Ford perfected the assembly line which made it possible to produce cars cheaply. Workers in an assembly line perform one operation before passing it on to the next person. Finished cars roll off the end of the assembly line.

Rearrange the parts on this assembly line to form words of things found on cars:

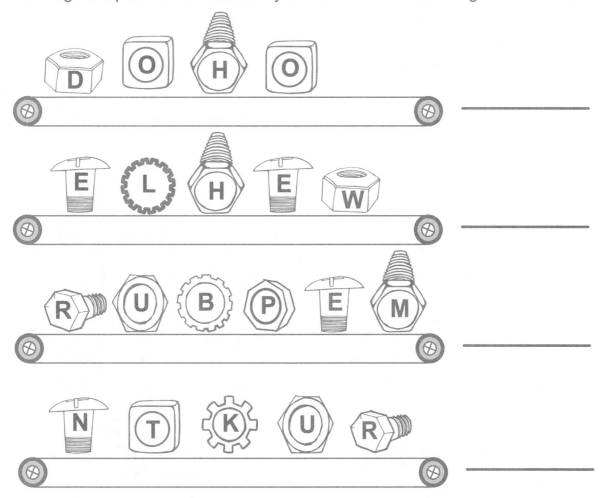

GARAGE SALE

What came first: the car or the garage?
The car of course! The word "garage" did not take on its current meaning until after 1900, when the first cars needed a place to park (and people needed a place to sell their used household items).

Rearrange these words for the answer to this riddle:
Q. When is a car not a car?

into when turns garage it a

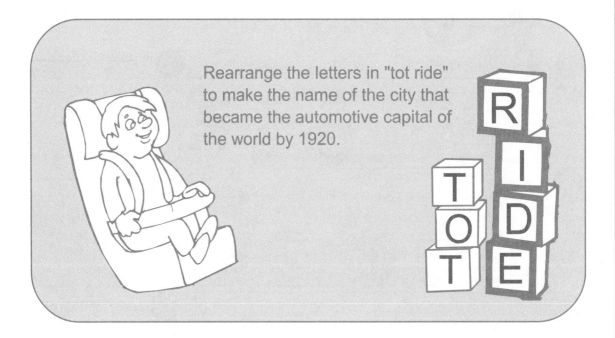

Rearrange the letters in "tot ride" to make the name of the city that became the automotive capital of the world by 1920.

Hidden Words

Find words that are hiding in these sentences. Hint: read between the words.
For example, this sentence has lion hidden in it: *Go to the deli on Main Street.*

Find a two-word engine part in this sentence:
Crisp Arkansas winds can flip luggage.

Find an explosion in this sentence:
Heard on the intercom: "bust

ions to reveal the secret."

Find a two-word engine part in this sentence:
Tofu elated the plump umpire

as he sat down for dinner.

Find a one-word engine part in this sentence:
This harp is toneless!

Find three engine liquids in this sentence:
The armadillo illustrations on the blazing

asphalt made the lizard swat erratically.

Find a force in this sentence:
The alligator questioned the lion.

Early Engines

Before 1900, this type of engine was more popular than gasoline engines in automobiles. To find the answer, put a letter in each box that corresponds to the starting letter of the pictures.

Electric Cars

Some car engines run on electricity, not gasoline. Can you untangle the crazy mess of electrical wires below? Draw a symbol in each empty box so that the wires connect to identical symbols.

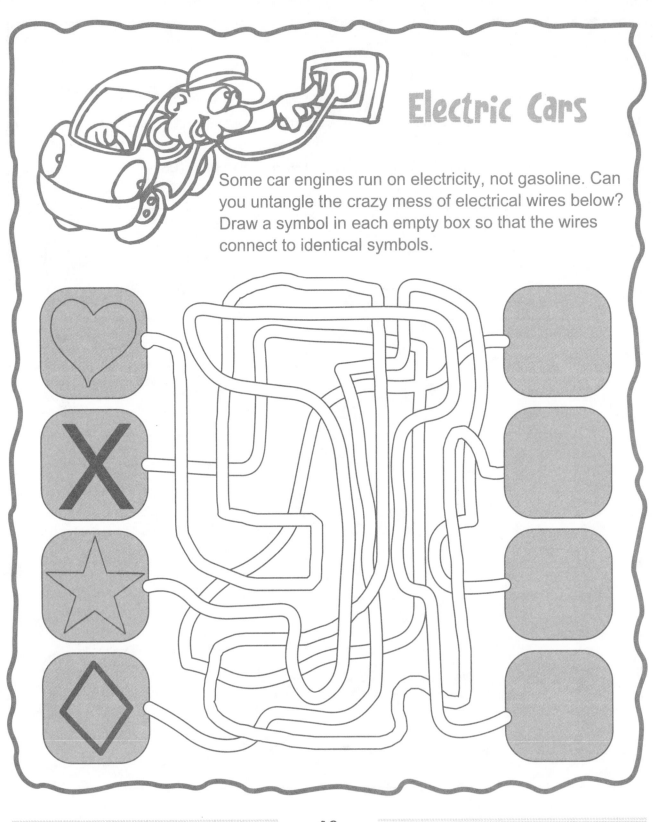

Changes

An engine changes energy into motion. In automobiles, this usually means changing gasoline into energy that moves the car.

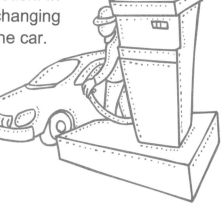

Can you convert one word into another word, one step at a time? Each step must be a real word, and must differ from the previous word by only one letter. There are many possible solutions, but try to use only the given number of steps.

Example:
BOY to MAN

B O Y
B A Y
M A Y
M A N

GEAR to WORK

G E A R
_ _ _ _
_ _ _ _
_ _ _ _
_ _ _ _
W O R K

GAS to CAR

G A S
_ _ _
_ _ _
C A R

SLOW to RACE

S L O W
_ _ _ _
_ _ _ _
_ _ _ _
_ _ _ _
R A C E

BOLT to NUTS

B O L T
_ _ _ _
_ _ _ _
_ _ _ _
_ _ _ _
N U T S

HORN to BEEP

H O R N
_ _ _ _
_ _ _ _
_ _ _ _
B E E P

Engine Letter

Cylinders in many engines make the shape of what letter? To find out, color in all of the pieces with two dots.

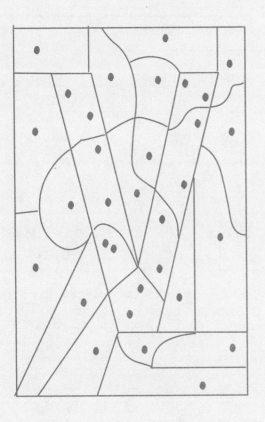

Gearing

If you turn the left gear the direction of the arrow, which way will the right gear move? Draw an arrow to show your answer.

Fuel Injection

For an engine to work properly, there must be an equal amount of fuel burned in each piston. Can you replace the question marks with numbers so that each piston has the same sum above it?

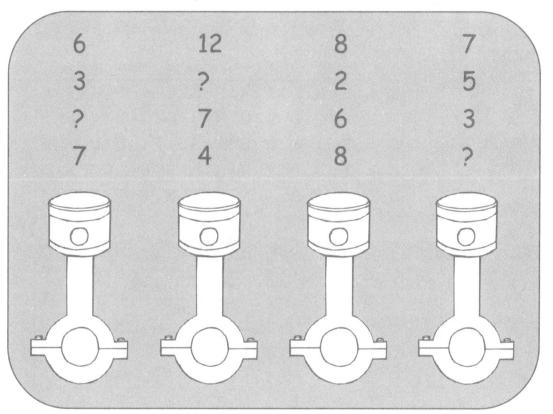

6	12	8	7
3	?	2	5
?	7	6	3
7	4	8	?

See if you can figure out the word below that is worn from age.
Hint: this engine part was replaced by fuel injection systems.

carburetor

Engine Parts

BELT
CAMSHAFT
CARBURETOR
COOLANT
CRANKSHAFT
CYLINDER
DISTRIBUTOR
EXHAUST
FAN
FILTER
FLYWHEEL
FUEL
GAS
GEARS
METAL
OIL PAN
PISTON
PULLEYS
PUMP
ROD
SPARK PLUG
STARTER
TUBES
WIRES

Find the names of engine parts in the list by looking up, down, across, backward, and diagonally in the letters below. Some letters may appear in more than one word. Remove any spaces in entries with multiple words.

```
L S E B U T K P C V A E K Y N
N Y R O U I U R J F T U Y E S
S E R I W M E T A L I C C S B
X L F J P T J N W B E L T R G
R L N C R A N K S H A F T A Z
Y U O A                 G S E I
F P T R                 U U G R
U S S B                 L A K E
N S I U                 P H D T
R G P R                 K X R U
S K X E C Y L I N D E R E E K
U D M T K T F A H S M A C Y A
X C O O L A N T W N A P L I O
A F P R O T U B I R T S I D Q
A W M X L E E H W Y L F U E L
```

Trivia ?

What toy was invented accidentally by an engineer who was playing with a spring?

Precision Engines

Engines are designed for precision. This means that one engine should be exactly the same as another engine. Can you find five differences between these two engines? The difference in color does not count as one of the five differences.

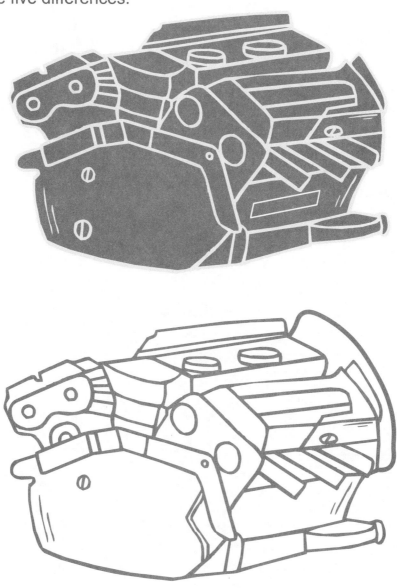

Engine Blanks

For these puzzles, determine the common word that can be combined with each of the three given words. The common word will be a part of an engine.

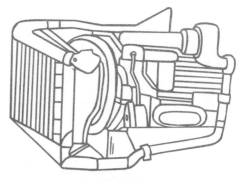

black _ _ _ _
_ _ _ _ buckle
asteroid _ _ _ _

fishing _ _ _
hot _ _ _
golden _ _ _

live _ _ _ _
high _ _ _ _
barbed _ _ _ _

_ _ _ paint
_ _ _ well
olive _ _ _

_ _ _ club
_ _ _ letter
attic _ _ _

Complete the sentences using these letters:
IEGORIOEHTARUFLRIATIDMLFRA
Each letter will be used once, so cross them off above as they are used.

A V8 engine has _ _ _ _ _ _ pistons.

_ _ _ is used to lubricate the engine.

In turbocharged engines, the _ _ _ coming into the engine is first pressurized to increase the power.

The _ _ _ _ _ _ _ quiets the noise from the explosions occurring in the engine.

Engines are cooled by water. The water is cooled when it flows through the

_ _ _ _ _ _ _ _.

Engine Jigsaw

Which of the missing pieces can be rotated to complete the engine?

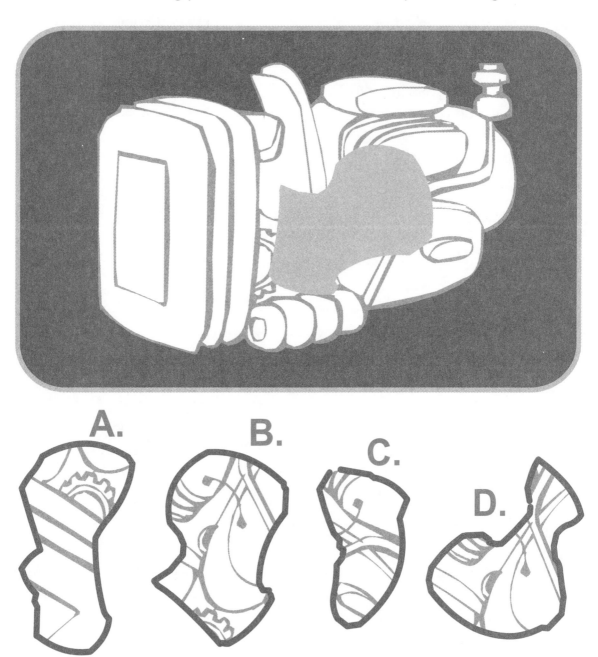

Four Strokes

Most cars today have a four-stroke internal combustion engine. Each cylinder goes through four strokes or stages to convert gasoline into motion. Can you figure out the correct order for the four stages? Number the boxes 1 to 4.

Do you know what year that the four-stroke engine was invented? To find out, count up every cent in these coins.

Combustion stroke: the gas explodes.

Intake stroke: air and gas is taken in.

Exhaust stroke: pushes out the burned gas.

Compression stroke: makes the explosion more powerful.

74 Quarters

2 Dimes

1 Nickel

1 Penny

Fractured Bumper Stickers

Sort through these pieces from six bumper stickers and see if you can figure out their messages.

1._____   4._____

2._____   5._____

3._____   6._____

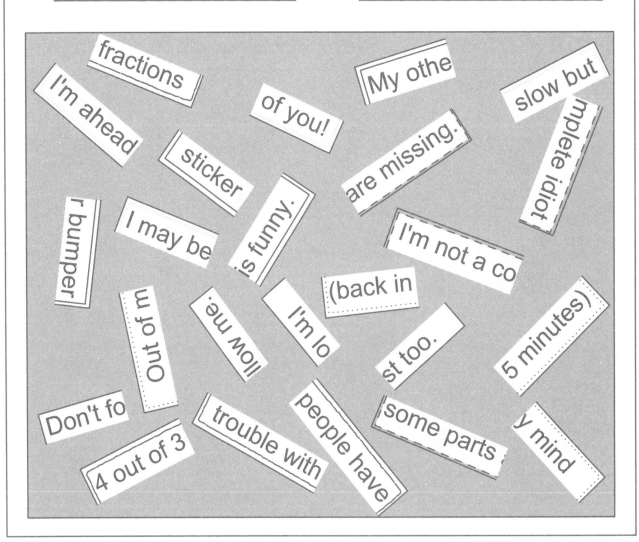

fractions

I'm ahead

My othe

slow but

of you!

are missing.

sticker

mplete idiot

r bumper

I may be

is funny.

I'm not a co

Out of m

(back in

5 minutes)

low me.

I'm lo

st too.

y mind

Don't fo

some parts

4 out of 3

trouble with

people have

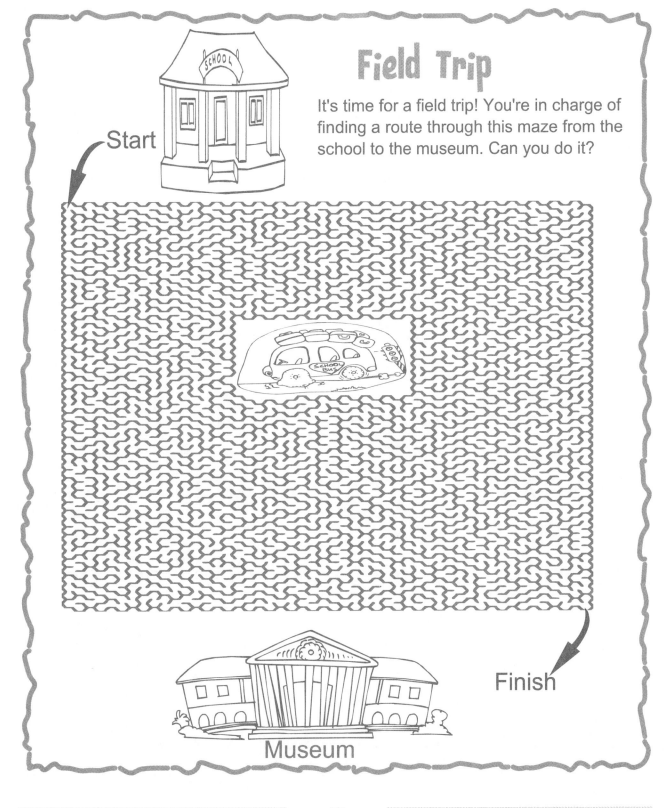

Field Trip

It's time for a field trip! You're in charge of finding a route through this maze from the school to the museum. Can you do it?

Start

Finish

Museum

California License Plate

California has more cars than any other state. Can you find the one license plate below that fits all of these rules:

1) It ends with an odd digit.
2) The sum of all the digits is less than 23.
3) It has a 5.
4) The first digit is less than the last digit.
5) It has six digits.

California	California	California	California
337318	190013	407695	314244

California	California	California	California
241941	995115	24720	721496

California	California	California	California
783678	973177	144563	848379

California	California	California	California
505614	668495	215605	367987

California	California	California	California
700555	900976	94561	983492

California	California	California	California
102206	16280	459403	86676

Road Map

Can you figure out what piece is missing from this old road map?

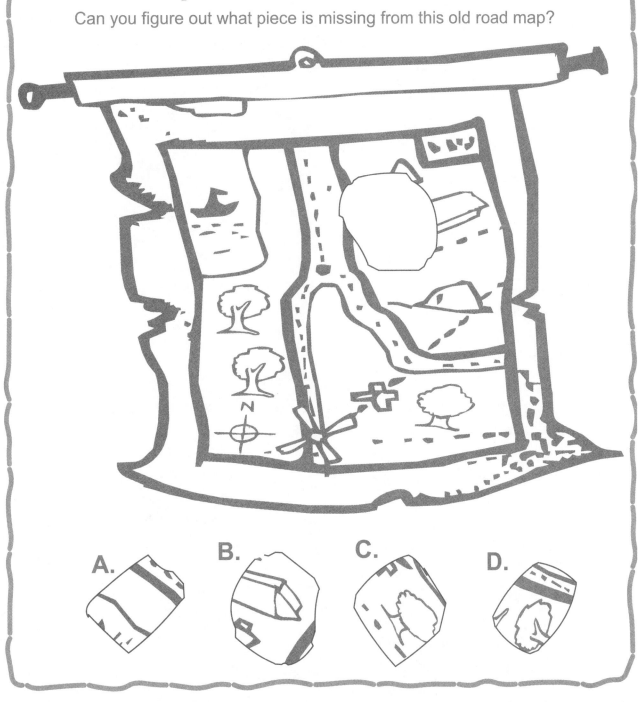

A.

B.

C.

D.

Crisscross Country

1. Indiana
2. Ohio
3. Illinois
4. Missouri
5. Kansas
6. New Mexico
7. Arizona
8. North Dakota
9. Iowa
10. Tennessee
11. Georgia
12. Alabama
13. Idaho
14. Wyoming
15. Iowa
16. Indiana

Find the dots in these states and connect them in order. You will make a piece of the flag.

Most states have slogans that they use to encourage tourism. Draw a line from each state to its slogan.

Live Free or Die   New Mexico
Great Potatoes. Tasty Destinations.   Washington
The Evergreen State   Alabama
The Islands of Aloha   New Hampshire
It's Good Being First   Delaware
Land of Enchantment   Hawaii
Greatest Snow on Earth   Utah
The Heart of Dixie   Idaho
The Grand Canyon State   Arizona
Fields of Opportunity   Iowa

Capital Anagrams

Anagrams are words formed by rearranging the letters in other words. For example, the letters in *teacher* can form "here cat". Can you rearrange the letters in these words to form the capitals of this list of states?

Arizona

Indiana

West Virginia

Tennessee

Alabama

New Mexico

Colorado

California

Arkansas

THORN LACES

TICKET ROLL

DR. EVEN

HALL VINES

NO METRO GYM

INLAID PIANOS

EAT FANS

SMART CANOE

HIP OXEN

Mileage

Vince's car can travel 36 miles for every gallon of gas. Can you figure out which of these places Vince can visit if he has two and a half gallons of gas? The trip will start from home and return home. The numbers are the miles between points on the map.

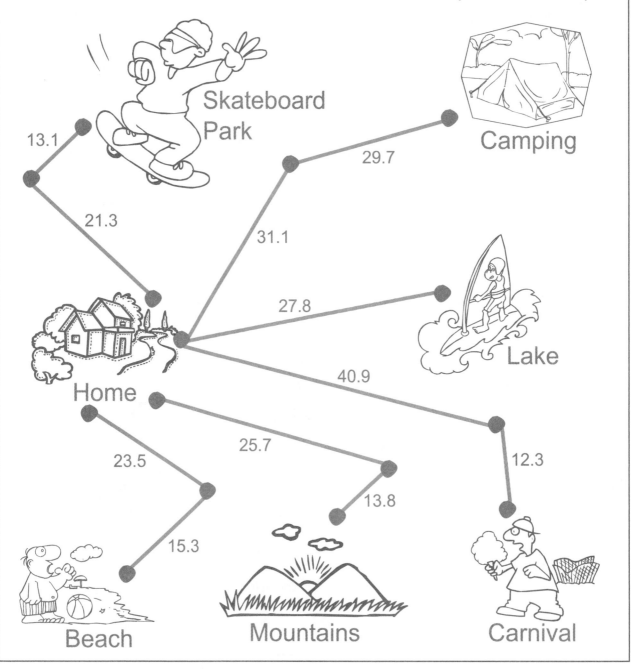

Road Scavenger Hunt

Here's a fun game to play next time you're on a road trip. See who can be the first in your car to find all of these things. Give a copy of this list to all of the passengers, or make up your own list.

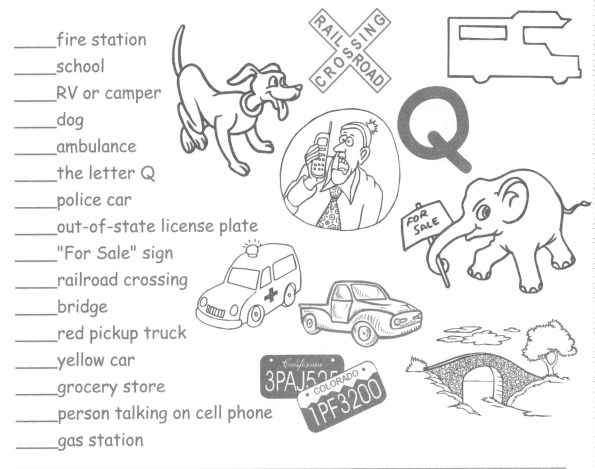

_____fire station
_____school
_____RV or camper
_____dog
_____ambulance
_____the letter Q
_____police car
_____out-of-state license plate
_____"For Sale" sign
_____railroad crossing
_____bridge
_____red pickup truck
_____yellow car
_____grocery store
_____person talking on cell phone
_____gas station

Can You Remember?

Try to remember all of the details of things you see on this page. Then turn to the next page and see if you can answer some questions from memory.

Do You Remember?

After carefully studying the previous page, see if you can answer these questions from memory. No peeking!

1. What animal has its tongue hanging out?
2. What states are the two license plates from?
3. Is the tree to the left or right of the bridge in the picture?
4. Is there a stop sign on the page?
5. What does the sign shaped like an X say?
6. What is carrying the "For Sale" sign?
7. Does the man's tie have stripes?
8. What direction is the pickup truck going on the page, left or right?
9. Is there an ambulance on the page?
10. What letter is directly above the "For Sale" sign?

Road Designer

Design a road to connect the nine dots with four straight lines without taking your pencil off the page. Hint: think outside the box.

Postcards

Each postcard has ten hidden numbers and letters.
Can you find all of them?

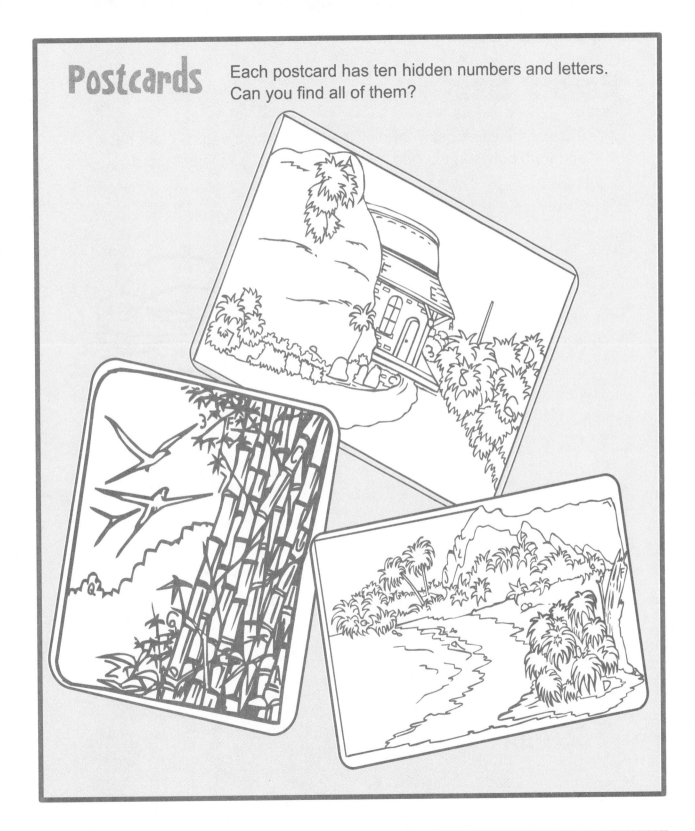

Road Riddles

Answer the clues below and fill the letters into the grid. Work back and forth between the grid and the clues until you figure it out.

A. Informal talk, especially on the Internet.

‾‾‾ ‾‾‾ ‾‾‾ ‾‾‾
11 12 13   4

B. A state of mind: happy, sad, angry, etc.

‾‾‾ ‾‾‾ ‾‾‾ ‾‾‾
10   6   7   1

C. Married to the Queen.

‾‾‾ ‾‾‾ ‾‾‾ ‾‾‾
 8   9 14 15

D. Lincoln lived in a ___ cabin.

‾‾‾ ‾‾‾ ‾‾‾
 5   2 18

E. A hotel or restaurant.

‾‾‾ ‾‾‾ ‾‾‾
16 17   3

What did the traffic light say to the car?

1B	2D	3E	4A '			
5D	6B	7B	8C	15C ▓	9C '	10B
11A	12A	13A	14C		16E	17E	18D

What would you call a country where everyone drives a pink car?
Break this shifty code to find the answer:

‾‾ ‾‾‾‾‾ ‾‾‾‾ ‾‾‾‾‾‾
B QJOL DBS OBUJPO

Factoid: Use the same code to find out the most popular color for cars made in 2004: ‾‾‾‾‾‾‾
TJMWFS

60

Rapid Response

A big emergency just happened! The police, ambulance, and fire department were all called. In what order will they arrive? Put a 1, 2, and 3 in the boxes.

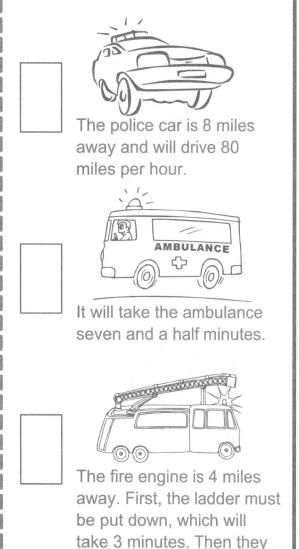

The police car is 8 miles away and will drive 80 miles per hour.

It will take the ambulance seven and a half minutes.

The fire engine is 4 miles away. First, the ladder must be put down, which will take 3 minutes. Then they will drive 60 miles per hour.

Divide the words into two groups by connecting the dots. One group should be "fast" words and the other group "slow" words. The puzzle has been started for you:

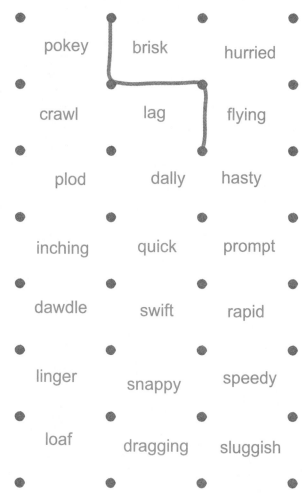

pokey   brisk   hurried

crawl   lag   flying

plod   dally   hasty

inching   quick   prompt

dawdle   swift   rapid

linger   snappy   speedy

loaf   dragging   sluggish

Fire Hose

Which fire hose should be connected to the hydrant so that fireman Frank will have water to put out the fire?

Here Spots!

Can you figure out the pattern that connects each dog to its fire engine?
Draw a line between matching pairs.

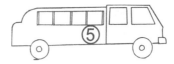

What Animals?

_____?_____ were useful in the early days of fire fighting because they were not afraid of the _____?_____ that pulled the fire engine. This dog would run out in front and clear the streets for the approaching fire engine.

Speedy Driver

This ambulance needs to get back to the hospital fast! Can you figure out the quickest route and how long it will take? Add up the numbers in a path to determine the total number of minutes.

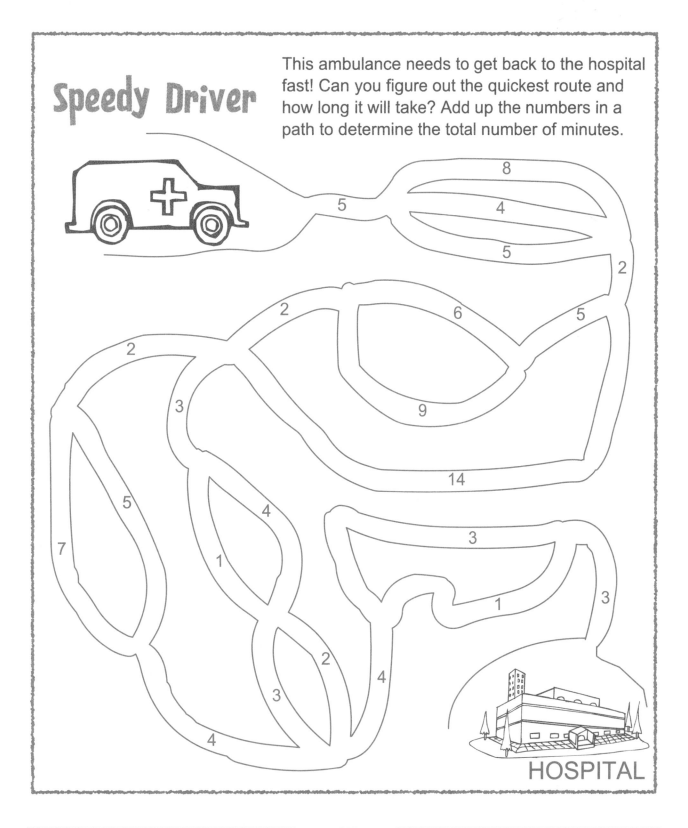

HOSPITAL

Catch a Thief

Officer Andy needs your help to catch the thief on this page. Here are the things we know about the thief:
1. He does not have a cane.
2. He is wearing a hat and tie.
3. He does not have dark glasses.
Who is the thief?

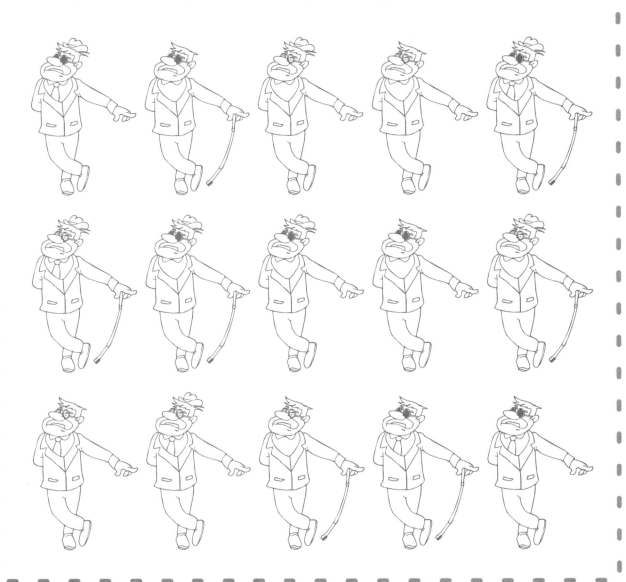

Clueless Crisis

See if you can fit all of these "crisis" words into this clueless crossword puzzle. Each word is used only once, so cross it off the list when you've found the spot for it. One of the words is done for you.

police
fire
ambulance
emergency
alarm
~~ladder~~
hydrant
extinguisher
safety
officer
badge
cop
firefighter
arrest
medic
hospital

LADDER

Ambulance Amusements

Answer the clues below and fill the letters into the grid. Work back and forth between the grid and the clues until you figure it out.

A. Continent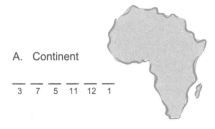

— — — — — —
3 7 5 11 12 1

B. Truck

— — — —
13 9 8 4

C. Peas in a

— — —
2 6 10

What do you call two doctors in an ambulance?

1A		2C	3A	4B	5A		6C	7A
8B	9B	10C	11A	12A	13B			

A father and son were in a car accident. One ambulance took the father to a hospital where he stayed for 3 days. Another ambulance took the son to a different hospital. When the son was taken into surgery the night of the accident, the surgeon said, "I can't operate on this patient because he is my son." How can this be?

Add a Siren

Add a siren to a vehicle and you get a police car, or an ambulance, or maybe a fire engine. Can you figure out what you get when you add the letters S-I-R-E-N to these letters, then rearrange?

For example, add a siren to H, rearrange the letters, and get a hallowed place.

S H R I N E

Add a siren to O, rearrange the letters, and get an elder.

_ _ _ _ _ _

Add a siren to M, rearrange the letters, and get ore extractors.

_ _ _ _ _ _

Add a siren to D and F, rearrange the letters, and get the keepers, not the weepers.

Add a siren to G, rearrange the letters, and get a vocalist.

_ _ _ _ _ _ _ _

_ _ _ _ _ _ _

Add a siren to D, rearrange the letters, and get people eating.

_ _ _ _ _ _

Safety Rules

Simple safety precautions can keep emergency vehicles away from your house! Can you complete these safety rules? Below is a list of the letters to use. Each letter will be used only once, so cross 'em off after you use 'em.

HORERBIAFEKESTUILASMINEXO
KEAMAVMIEWTEECRSWTSTYGAG

This helps put out fires: _ _ _ _ _ _ _ _ _|_|_ _

Riding these brings more kids to the hospital emergency room than any other sport: _ _ _|_|_

Your house should have one of these on every floor to prevent fires: _ _ _ _ _ _   _|_|_ _ _

Never put metal in this appliance: |_|_ _ _ _ _ _ _ _

Never touch anything electrical if you are _|_|_

Always re-latch this to protect young brothers and sisters from danger: _ _ _ _|_|_   _ _ _ _

When you are done, read the letters in the boxes to reveal the smartest thing you can wear while riding a bike or skateboard.

Hardware Burglar Chase

He has struck again! Direct the police car through these wild roads and catch the hardware burglar.

Antique Fire Engines

Horse-drawn steam fire engines were used
before the gasoline engine was invented.
What shadow exactly matches this antique
fire engine?

What famous person formed the
first fire department in America?

hint:

Chapter 7

Service Stations

Speedy Mart

See if you can find the five things that you can buy at the Speedy Mart service station. To find them, take one letter from each column moving left to right. Each letter can be used only once, so cross them off as you go. One item has been done for you.

G A M
C O F A
C O N F I
S U O D E E
C O D K X E S

1. _ _ _ _ _ _ _ 22 cents
2. _ _ _ _ _ _ 37 cents
3. C A N D Y 7 cents
4. _ _ _ _ _ 25 cents
5. _ _ _ 14 cents

Here is the amount each kid spent buying the five items. What items did they buy?

Jake spent 39 cents.

Sally spent 29 cents.

Ronald spent 46 cents.

Check Your Oil!

Without oil, the metal parts of an engine would grind together and tear themselves apart. Read the clues below and see if you can complete the words that all contain the letters O-I-L.

The top layer of the earth, where plants grow

? O I L

Don't forget to flush!

I L ? O I L ? ?

A bundle of rope

? O I L

Milk out of the refrigerator will...

? ? O I L L ?

Changes water to steam

O I L

A thin sheet of aluminum

? O I L

Who Broke It?

If **none** of these statements from the kids is true, then who broke the car?

Lisa: The name of the person who broke the car starts with the letter M.

Mark: I broke the car.

Justin: I did not break the car.

Mike: Sally broke the car.

Sally: I know nothing about cars.

Frank: A girl broke the car.

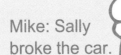

Age? (All of these statements are true!)
Lisa is five years older than Mike. Frank is two years older than Sally. Mike will be six years old next year. Sally is three years younger than Lisa. How old is Frank?

Tire Rotation

Changing the position of each tire on a car can help the tread to wear more evenly. How many ways can you put four different tires onto four axles?

Fill It Up With What?

Outside of North America, what do people in English-speaking countries call gasoline? To find out, figure out the missing letter in each column, then read all the missing letters across. Each missing letter completes a three-letter word reading from top to bottom.

A	J	I	C	D	E
E	T	S	Y	T	F

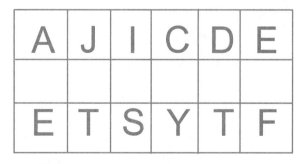

Doctor Ottoman's Barn

Can you figure out the names of the things shown on this page? They all belong to Doctor Ottoman, our mad scientist who likes to work on cars. See if you can find the names of all these things in the letters on Doctor Ottoman's Barn.

B _ _ _ _ _ _ _

N _ _

P _ _ _ _ _

R _ _ _

L _ _ _ _ _

B _ _ _

W _ _ _ _

H _ _ _

G _ _ _ _

H _ _ _

W _ _ _ _ _

C Y
X S W A
W Y H R L M
Y R E T T A B G
E E L K L D E B
L N L O O D T G
I C U O B E U L
H P H O R N
E P O R
X B

To find the words, look up, down, across, backward, and diagonally.
Some letters may appear in more than one word.

Find Andy's Key

Andy just had his car fixed and wants his key back. Which key should Sam hand him? Andy's key is the only one on this page with no matching pair.

Did you know that maps used to be given away free at service stations? These old maps have been ripped into two pieces. Draw a line connecting the left side to the right side for each map.

Ask for Directions

Follow these directions and see if you can answer the questions that follow. Here's a hint: if you're going east and turn left then you will be going north.

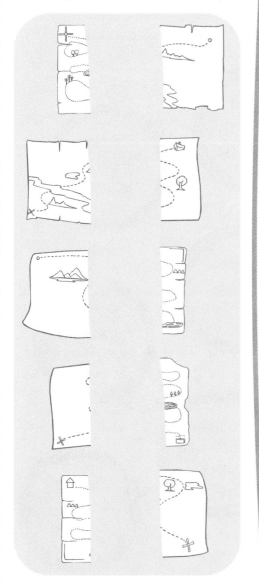

Drive south for one mile.

Turn left and drive for five miles.

Turn left and drive for three miles.

Turn right and drive for four miles.

Turn right and drive for two miles.

How far will you be from the starting point?

What direction will you be from the starting point?

Tire Balancing Act

To run smoothly, tires must be balanced.
Balance the tires on this page by
crossing out the one misspelled word
found in each wheel. If you need to, use
a dictionary to check the spellings.

usualy
shepherd
biscuit

vacum
describe
necessary

interrupt
neighbor
scarey

really
mischief
privlege

seperate
immediately
knowledge

physical
vilage
challenge

rhythm
recomend
schedule

athlete
calendar
suprise

changing
labratory
either

definite
accidentally
disapoint

similar
beginning
fourty

benefit
conveinent
disease

Matt's Boxes

Auto mechanic Matt has a habit of arranging parts in sets of nine boxes. Here is an example of the part counts for each box:

8	3	4
1	5	9
6	7	2

Notice these things about the part counts:
1. Each number from 1 to 9 is used exactly once.
2. The total sum of each row, column, and diagonal is the same.

This is the way Matt likes to arrange his parts! Can you help him determine the part counts for the empty boxes so they follow the rules above?

2		6
9	5	1
	3	

	9	4
		3
6	1	8

4		2
	5	
8		6

4	3	8
9		
2		

	7	
1		9
	3	

6		
7		
2		

Four Wheel Drive

About 300 million tires are made each year worldwide. Can you find the four identical tires on this page?

Chapter 8

Construction Vehicles

Mathemagical Roof

Roofer Ralph has put shingles on this house that he hauled with his truck. Now he needs your help to complete this roof. For each empty shingle (or box) below, enter the sum of the two numbers beneath it on either corner. One example is already done (5+1=6). Complete all of the shingles to the very top.

Tractor Pull

Tractors are used for all kinds of serious work on the farm and in construction. Sometimes, just for fun, tractors play tug-of-war to see which one can pull the other. In this puzzle, the winning tractor is the one with the higher number. Solve these equations to determine each tractor's number, then circle each winner.

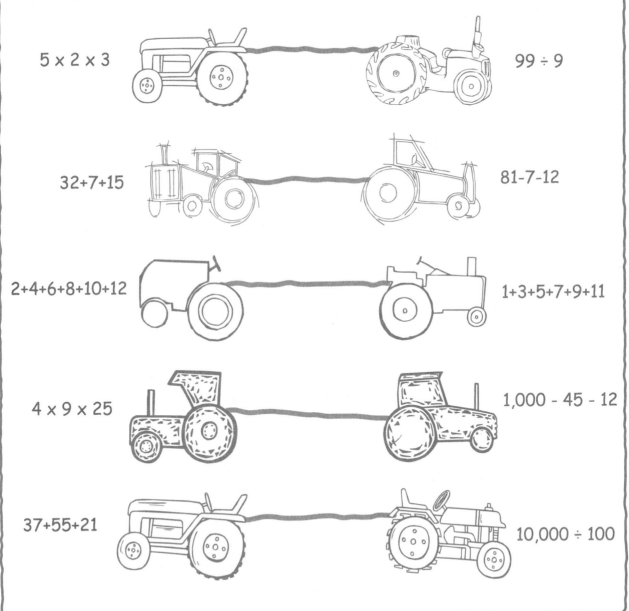

$5 \times 2 \times 3$ $99 \div 9$

$32+7+15$ $81-7-12$

$2+4+6+8+10+12$ $1+3+5+7+9+11$

$4 \times 9 \times 25$ $1,000 - 45 - 12$

$37+55+21$ $10,000 \div 100$

All Mixed Up

Uh oh! These cement mixers scrambled the letters. Can you un-mix the letters and figure out the words? Hint: the words are all construction tools that you can see on this page.

Smileys Everywhere

Can you circle all 30 smileys hidden in this junky construction site?

Give a Lift

Copy each of the nine squares from the next page into this grid.
The letters and numbers tell you where each square belongs.

	A	B	C
1			
2			
3			

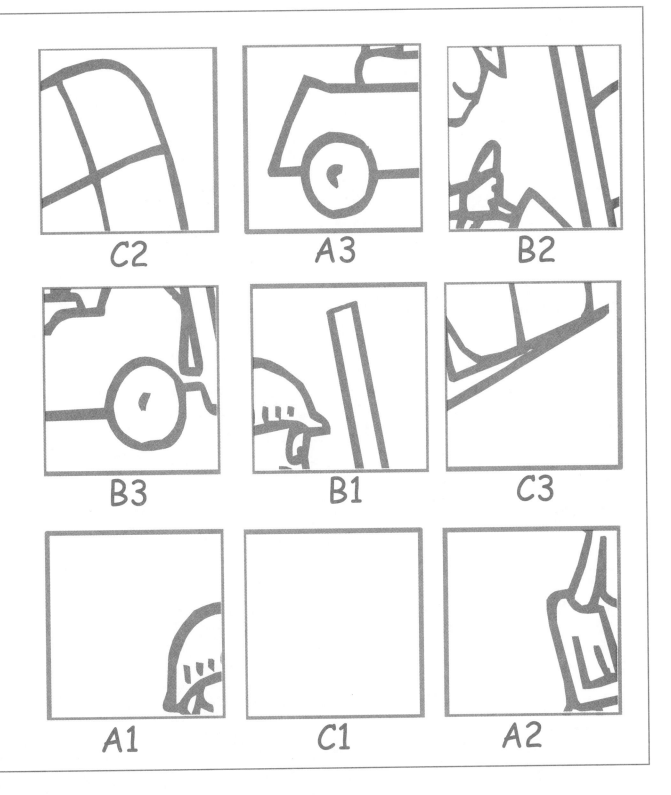

C2

A3

B2

B3

B1

C3

A1

C1

A2

Wireman Wayne

Wireman Wayne carries a giant spool of wire in his truck.
Can you help him untangle the wires and answer this riddle?
Fill in each blank with the letter at the other end of the wire.

What kind of car does an electrician drive?

A ◯ ◯ ◯ ◯ ◯ WAGON

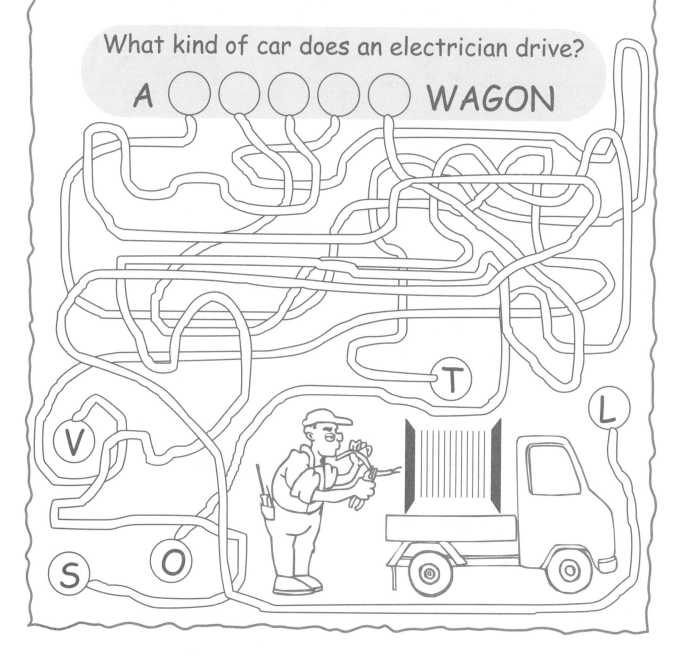

A Site to See

Can you find ten differences between these two construction sites?

Letter Bulldozers

Using letters in the word BULLDOZERS, you can make the words RED and DOLL and many others. Can you find at least twenty words contained in BULLDOZERS?

1. _____
2. _____
3. _____
4. _____
5. _____
6. _____
7. _____
8. _____
9. _____
10. _____

11. _____
12. _____
13. _____
14. _____
15. _____
16. _____
17. _____
18. _____
19. _____
20. _____

Construction Crossword

ACROSS

2 the four sides of a room
4 useful for digging
6 useful for making holes in wood
8 hit these with a hammer
12 the top of a building
13 its cables lift heavy objects

15

17 hard _ _ _
18 wood sawed into boards
19 a coat that protects and colors
20 a step on a ladder

DOWN

1 useful for pounding
3 useful for cutting
4 overlaps and covers the roof

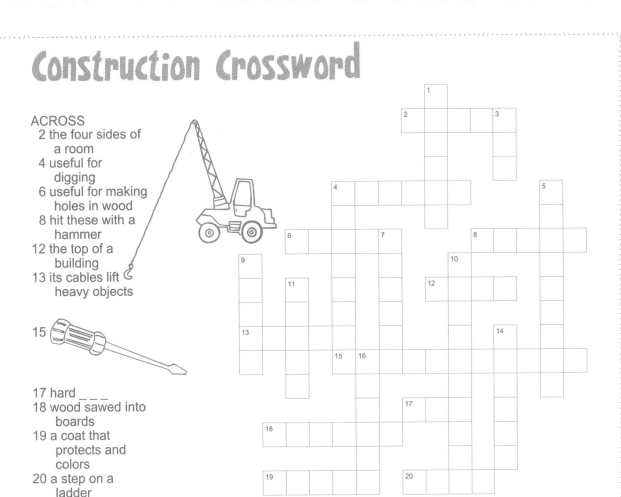

5

7 you can climb up this

9 dump _ _ _ _ _

10 the base on which a building stands
11 useful for holding two pieces of wood together

14 _ _ _ _ _ _
truck

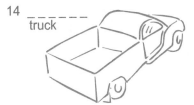

16 _ _ _ _ _ _
mixer

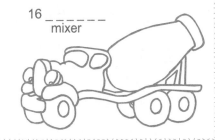

Gravel Movers

These two dumptrucks hold exactly 5 tons and 3 tons of gravel. You need to haul 4 tons of gravel to the construction site. How can you measure the gravel without a scale? Hint: gravel can be moved between the dumptrucks.

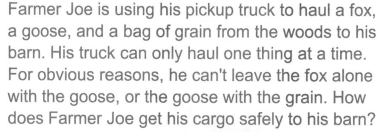

Farmer Joe

Farmer Joe is using his pickup truck to haul a fox, a goose, and a bag of grain from the woods to his barn. His truck can only haul one thing at a time. For obvious reasons, he can't leave the fox alone with the goose, or the goose with the grain. How does Farmer Joe get his cargo safely to his barn?

nICE Words

Of course the ice cream truck has the word ICE on it. Can you figure out these words that contain the letters I-C-E?

_ _ _ I C E

_ _ I C E

_ I C E

_ _ I C E

_ I C E

_ _ I C E

_ _ I C E

Favorite Flavors

Find all of the flavors in this ice cream cone by looking up, down, across, backward, and diagonally. Some letters may appear in more than one word.

```
            H D I
        T U N O C O C O B
      R D F T F J V T A T G I G
    M J F K U V O T N R O E F A C W Q
    L E M O N H T P I S T A C H I O A B P
  N W V O L F C O M V L G I S S C F L I M E
  Y R R E B W A R T S E K H H P R F N B O Q
G N A Z B L U E B E R R Y R Q E B E U L B B K
K D A Y D J P P R F V A N I L L A E T I Z B S
Q N H C C I P C P N T O K B K Z P N H R T O Z T L
A S I J A E T A L O C O H C A P T A B T R U G J R
P D U H P G P H D A J M X Q L O M N I D D Y B W J
L X W O T Z K W I K R G C H E R R Y A A S B X D J A Y
```

VANILLA

CHOCOLATE

STRAWBERRY

BANANA

PEACH

COFFEE

RASPBERRY

CHERRY

LEMON

BLUEBERRY

PINEAPPLE

COCONUT

PISTACHIO

HAZELNUT

MINT

PEPPERMINT

LIME

BUTTERSCOTCH

PECAN

WALNUT

Frosty Riddles

Every frozen treat from this ice cream truck comes with a riddle printed on its package. Use the code on the side of the truck to find out the answers.

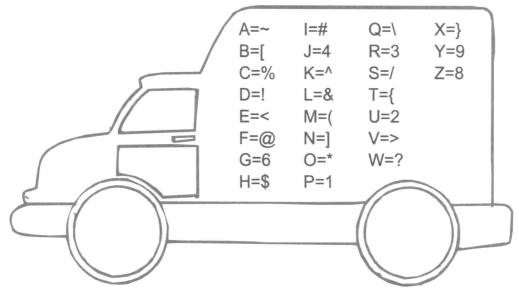

A=~	I=#	Q=\	X=}
B=[	J=4	R=3	Y=9
C=%	K=^	S=/	Z=8
D=!	L=&	T={	
E=<	M=(	U=2	
F=@	N=]	V=>	
G=6	O=*	W=?	
H=$	P=1		

What gets wetter the more it dries?

~ {*?<&

Why did the lion eat the tightrope walker?

/* $< %*2&! $~>< ~ [~&~]%<! (<~&

What do you get from a pampered cow?

/1*#&<! (#&^

What do you get when you cross a snowman with a vampire?

@3*/{[#{<

Where do snowmen keep their money?

#] ~ /]*? [~]^

When is a door not a door?

?$<] #{ #/ ~4~3

Ice Cream Across America

Uncle Sam is driving his ice cream truck from the state of Washington to Florida. Can you help him find the path?

START

FINISH

A Sweet Treat

It's rhyme time! Ice cream man Dan is giving out a sweet treat to everyone who can figure out these rhyming word pairs. One is done for you to get you started.

What is peanut butter's stinky partner?

S M E L L Y   J E L L Y

What is a dull taxi?

_ _ _ _   _ _ _

What do you call a wheat railroad?

_ _ _ _ _   _ _ _ _ _

What is an angry father?

_ _ _   _ _ _

What is a 50% chuckle?

_ _ _ _   _ _ _ _ _

What is a false serpent?

_ _ _ _   _ _ _ _ _

What is a cheerful father?

_ _ _ _ _   _ _ _ _ _

What do you call a soggy tent area?

_ _ _ _   _ _ _ _

What are some very odd coins in your pocket?

_ _ _ _ _ _ _   _ _ _ _ _ _

What is a hat for afternoon slumber?

_ _ _   _ _ _

What is a doggy kiss?

_ _ _ _ _ _   _ _ _ _ _ _

What is a frightening milk provider?

_ _ _ _ _   _ _ _ _ _

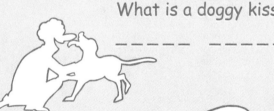

What is a crazy kid?

_ _ _ _   _ _ _ _ _

What are pleasant rodents?

_ _ _ _   _ _ _ _

What do you call a better-looking personal instructor?

_ _ _ _ _   _ _ _ _ _

What do you call a tire bargain?

_ _ _ _ _   _ _ _ _

The Next Ice Cream Bar

Can you guess which ice cream bar will be given after the first two?

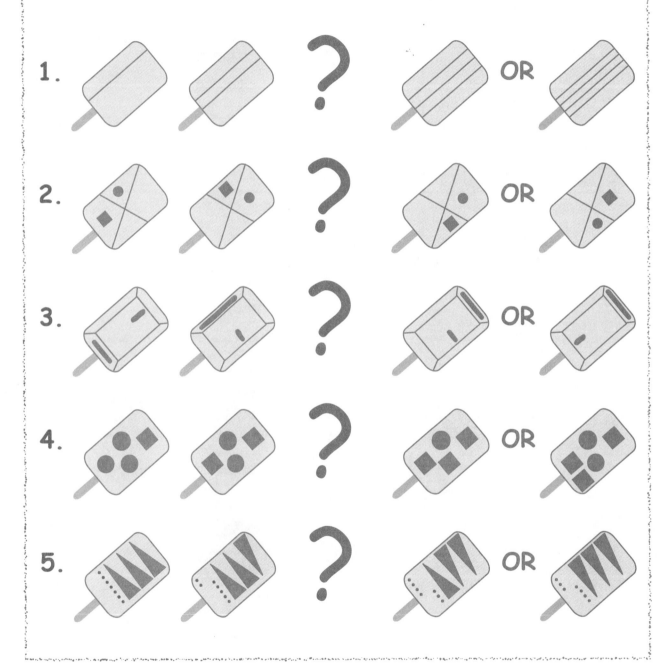

Sharing

Olivia, Louis, and Paul want to buy a 30-cent ice cream bar to share. If they put all of their money together will it be enough? How much money does each person have?

Olivia and Louis together have a total of 18 cents.
Louis and Paul together have a total of 23 cents.
Paul and Olivia together have a total of 19 cents.

Ice Cream Trivia

What is the most popular ice cream topping?

What is the most popular ice cream flavor?

Who was the first U.S. President to eat ice cream?

The first hand-cranked ice cream freezer was patented in what year: 1848, 1904, or 1955?

Sweet Menu

This ice cream truck will serve you a scoop of ice cream with one topping. How many different combinations of flavors and toppings are there? Here is the menu:

FLAVORS (pick one)
Vanilla
Chocolate
Strawberry
Banana
Coconut
Walnut

TOPPINGS (pick one)
Nuts
Cherries
Caramel
Fudge

For the Very Hungry

This ice cream truck also serves a special treat called The Ice Cream Pyramid. Each layer has one less scoop of ice cream until there is only one scoop at the very top. For example, here is the ice cream pyramid with three scoops at the base:

How many total scoops will there be for an ice cream pyramid with five scoops at the base? It might help to draw a picture of the pyramid.

Exact Change

You must use exact change to buy these treats from the ice cream truck.

Which treat can be bought using the fewest number of coins?

Which treat requires the most number of coins?

 61¢

 63¢

 95¢

 87¢

 29¢

 18¢

 68¢

You can use as many of these coins as needed, but always use the fewest number possible:

 25¢ 10¢ 5¢   1¢

Candy Please

The ice cream truck also sells candy!
Can you figure out what these kids want
based on the display below?

Jill wants the candy in the middle of the row without a lollipop.

Frank wants the candy that is on the display just twice.

Emma wants a candy not found in the second row, but not gum.

Erica wants the piece of candy found between a hard candy and a lollipop.

Carlos wants the candy that appears twice in a row.

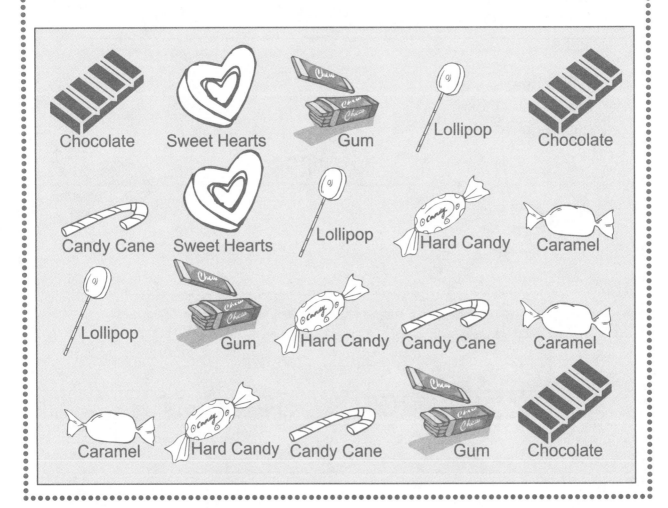

Appendix

Fun Web Sites

www.funbrain.com
Brainy (but really fun) games for kids of all ages.
Play MathCar Racing to see how good you can drive.

www.chevroncars.com
Collect cars online, play car games, and learn new
things about cars at this fun Web site.

www.funster.com
Compete against friends at this Web site with
multiplayer word games and other puzzles.
Created by the author of this book!

www.bonus.com
Chocked full of fun games of all types.
Check out the racing games found in the
sports section.

www.monstertruckracing.com
Filled with extremely cool pictures of monster
trucks in action.

www.funschool.com
The emphasis is definitely on fun at this Web site
with a variety of games for every grade.

www.ottoclub.org
Join Otto for fun activities about autos and car
safety. From the Northern California AAA.

www.aaa-calif.com/otto
More fun with Otto, including online coloring and
games. From the Southern California AAA.

www.sparky.org
Brought to you by Sparky the fire dog. Includes an
entire section devoted to fire trucks.

www.hotwheels.com
Free games and more cool stuff with scorching
fast cars.

www.cedysworld.com
Build a soapbox car and go on adventures around
the world at this kid's Web site from Mercedes-
Benz.

Games to Play in the Car

*Here are some fun games to play
the next time you're on the road.*

The Alphabet Game
Start with the letter A. When a player sees the letter in a sign or on a license plate they point to it and
say the letter. Once a letter has been pointed out,
no one else can use it. The player who found the letter moves on to the next letter (B, C, and so on). The
first player to go from A to Z is the winner.

Name That Tune
One person hums a favorite song. It can be a popular
tune or perhaps a TV show theme song. The first person to correctly guess the tune hums the next song.

Who Am I?
One person states that they are either a person, a
place, or a thing. Other players take turns asking
yes/no questions until someone guesses what the
person is. The player who guesses correctly gets
to be the next person, place, or thing.

License Plates
Find license plates for all 50 states. This game is a
favorite for really long trips, or keep a running list
in your car.

Eye Spy
A player spots an object and gives one clue about
it. For example, "I spy something shiny." After all
of the other players take a guess, another clue is
given. The first person to guess correctly gets to
spy the next object.

Acronym
See who can come up with the funniest acronym
from the letters on a license plate. For example, if
the license plate is 8MNG32 the acronym could be
"My Nice Gorilla", or something even funnier.

Colors
Assign each player a common car color like blue,
silver, or white. See who can be the first person to
find ten cars or trucks with their color.

The EVERYTHING KIDS' Cars and Trucks Puzzle and Activity Book

page vi • Find the Pictures

5   2   6

9   8   7

1   3   4

page 2 • Stopwatch Mysteries

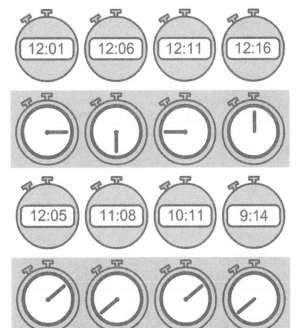

12:01   12:06   12:11   12:16

12:05   11:08   10:11   9:14

page 3 • Crazy Driver

C: L,R,L,L,L,R,R,L,L,L,R,L

page 4 • Fast Cars

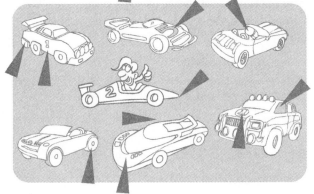

page 5 • Fruit Race

Racecar 7 Wins. (But not by much!)

 =64 points

 =65 points

Puzzle Answers

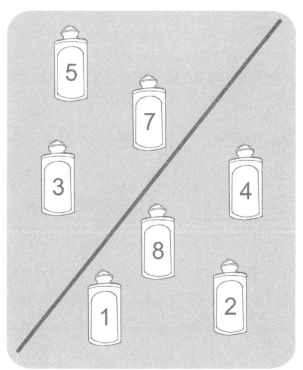

2	9	3	8
+1	-7	+6	-5
3	**2**	**9**	**3**
+4	-1	-8	+6
7	**1**	**1**	**9**
-5	+4	+3	-9
2	**5**	**4**	**0**
+6	-2	+5	+4
8	**3**	**9**	**4**
-7	+6	-4	+5
1	**9**	**5**	**9**

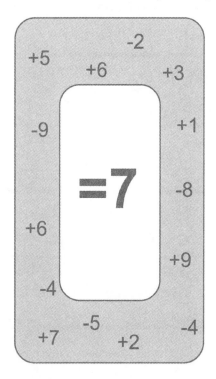

111

The EVERYTHING KIDS' Cars and Trucks Puzzle and Activity Book

page 8 • Race to the Checkered Flag

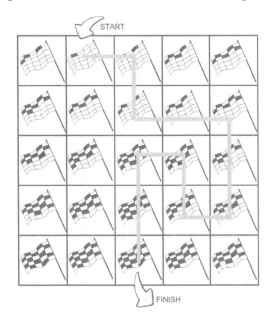

page 9 • Racing Code

1. __F__ __A__ __S__ __T__

2. __S__ __P__ __E__ __E__ __D__ __Y__

3. __R__ __A__ __P__ __I__ __D__

4. __S__ __W__ __I__ __F__ __T__

5. __Q__ __U__ __I__ __C__ __K__

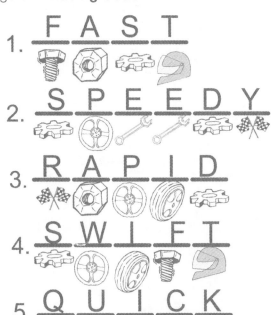

page 10 • Racing Rhymes

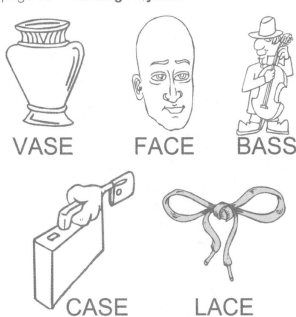

VASE   FACE   BASS

CASE   LACE

page 11 • Start Your Engines

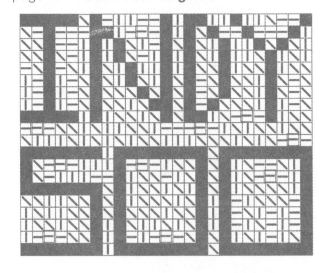

Puzzle Answers

page 12 • An aMAZEing Race

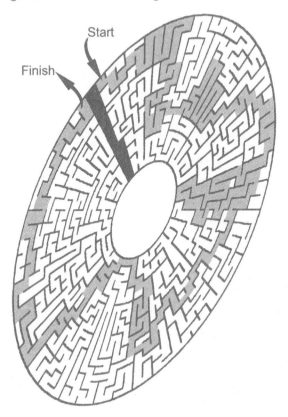

page 15 • Numbers Convoy

page 16 • Special Delivery

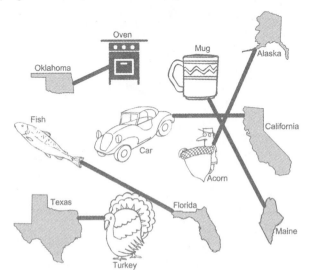

page 14 • Monster's Truck

The EVERYTHING KIDS' Cars and Trucks Puzzle and Activity Book

page 17 • **Twisty Routes**

page 19 • **Postman**

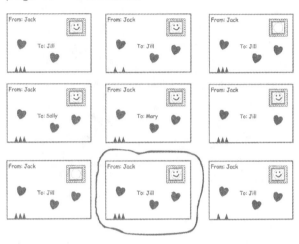

page 18 • **Circle Movers**

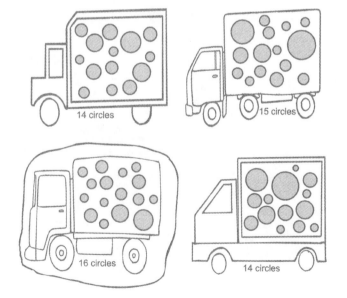

page 20 • **Wear and Tear**

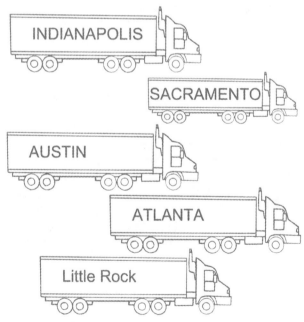

Puzzle Answers

page 21 • **Flying Wheels**

1: EAGERRAE

2: YRYBCCAG

3: BBBEATAR

4: ZZUDCZDK

Answer:_A GARBAGE TRUCK_____

page 22 • **Scrambled Groceries**

BREAD

FLOUR

EGGS

MILK

SUGAR

CEREAL

RICE

page 23 • **10–4 Good Buddy!**

Q. WHAT IS BIG, WHITE, GIVES MILK, AND HAS ONE HORN?

A. A MILK TRUCK.

page 24 • **What's Missing**

S

E

M

I

page 26 • Horseless Pioneers

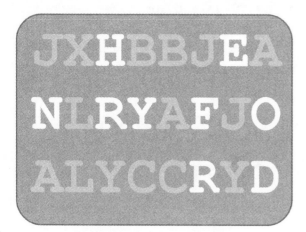

HENRY FORD

page 28 • A Horse of Course

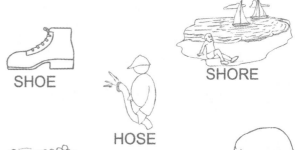

SHOE

SHORE

HOSE

ORE

ROSE

page 26 • Wheels Turning

Approximately how old is the oldest wheel ever found by archaeologists?
(C) five thousand years old

page 29 • Striped Automobiles

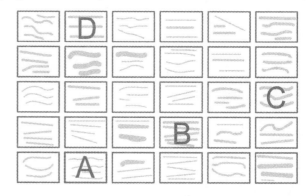

page 27 • Glove Compartment

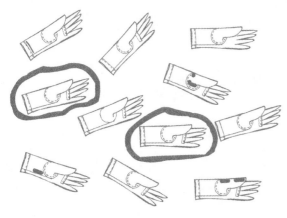

Puzzle Answers

page 30 • **Model T for Tiger**

This car has a toothy grill: Model Alligator
This car is huggable: Model Bear
This car has a hump: Model Camel
This car waddles: Model Duck
This car has a long trunk: Model Elephant
This car can swim: Model Fish
This car is for tall people: Model Giraffe
This car is enormous: Model Hippopotamus
This car has scaly upholstery: Model Iguana
This car is very fast: Model Jaguar
This car really jumps: Model Kangaroo
This car can roar: Model Lion
This car can swing: Model Monkey
This car could be called Salamander: Model Newt
WHO would want this car?: Model Owl
This car can talk: Model Parrot
This car can fly: Model Quail
This car helps Santa deliver: Model Reindeer
This car is very slow: Model Snail

page 31 • **Safari**

The Hippopotamus has wandered away.

page 32 • **Famous Inventors**

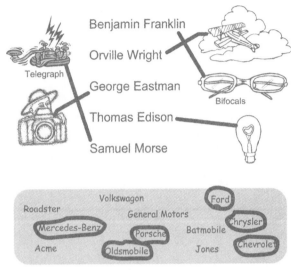

page 33 • **Wheels Go Round**

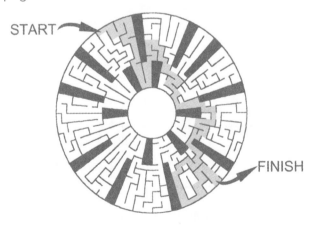

A **CRANK** was turned to start the original horseless carriages.

117

page 34 • Early Car Biz

```
R X K I D D E R A C E N E S F
E X E S S E L R E E P O Z D A
S M R L O T S I R B M S I R L
I D O E P L U H O C K D M A C
A L N R D M A Y A D E U M K O
K Z L A T L A M V U C H E C N
B A Z E L S E T T E U Q R A M
E F Z A W R M F R S S I M P R
Y L D L O X E O G E O A A R O
M A T N A B A V L N V K N A S
Y N L L O C O M O B I L E T D
V D I G O O D S P E E D A T N
X E X C A L I B U R L X V C I
C R O S L E Y E L G I N P Z W
H S A N A R N O L T U C K E R
```

page 36 • Garage Sale

Q. When is a car not a car?
A. When it turns into a garage.

page 36 • Tot Ride

TOT RIDE=**DETROIT**

page 38 • Hidden Words

spark plug
combustion
fuel pump
piston
oil, gas, water
torque

page 35 • Assembly Line

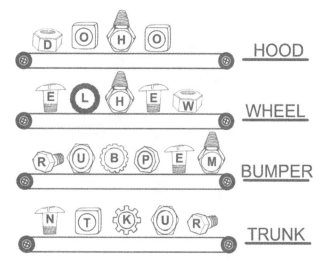

HOOD
WHEEL
BUMPER
TRUNK

page 39 • Early Engines

S
T
E
A
M

Puzzle Answers

page 40 • **Electric Cars**

page 41 • **Changes**

**There are many possible answers.
Here are our answers:**

SLOW	GEAR	GAS
SLOT	PEAR	WAS
SOOT	PEAK	WAR
ROOT	PERK	CAR
ROOK	PORK	
ROCK	WORK	HORN
RACK		TORN
RACE		TERN
	BOLT	TEEN
	COLT	BEEN
	COOT	BEEP
	COOS	
	COTS	
	CUTS	
	NUTS	

page 42 • **Engine Letter**

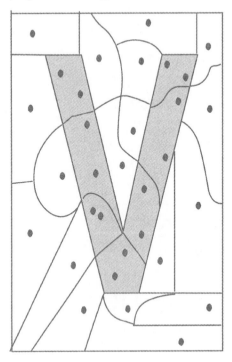

page 42 • **Gearing**

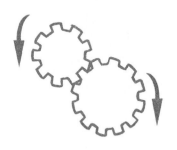

page 43 • Fuel Injection

6	12	8	7
3	1	2	5
8	7	6	3
7	4	8	9

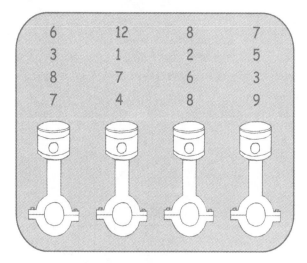

carburetor

page 44 • Trivia

The **Slinky** was invented by a naval engineer who worked on engines.

page 45 • Precision Engines

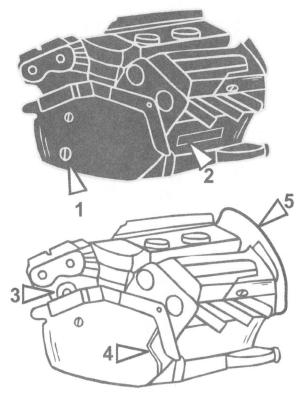

page 44 • Engine Parts

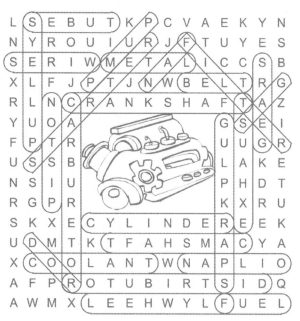

L S E B U T K P C V A E K Y N
N Y R O U I U R J F T U Y E S
S E R I W M E T A L I C C S B
X L F J P T J N W B E L T R G
R L N C R A N K S H A F T A Z
Y U O A G S E I
F P T R U U G R
U S S B L A K E
N S I U P H D T
R G P R K X R U
S K X E C Y L I N D E R E E K
U D M T K T F A H S M A C Y A
X C O O L A N T W N A P L I O
A F P R O T U B I R T S I D Q
A W M X L E E H W Y L F U E L

Puzzle Answers

page 46 •
Engine Blanks

black **BELT**
BELT buckle
asteroid **BELT**

fishing **ROD**
hot **ROD**
golden **ROD**

live **WIRE**
high **WIRE**
barbed **WIRE**

OIL paint
OIL well
olive **OIL**

FAN club
FAN letter
attic **FAN**

A V8 engine has **EIGHT** pistons.

OIL is used to lubricate the engine.

In turbocharged engines, the **AIR** coming into the engine is first pressurized to increase the power.

The **MUFFLER** quiets the noise from the explosions occurring in the engine.

Engines are cooled by water. The water is cooled when it flows through the **RADIATOR**.

page 47 • **Engine Jigsaw**

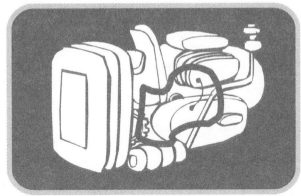

B.

page 48 • **Four Strokes**

3 Combustion stroke: the gas explodes.

1 Intake stroke: air and gas is taken in.

4 Exhaust stroke: pushes out the burned gas.

2 Compression stroke: makes the explosion more powerful.

The four-stroke engine was invented in **1876**.

page 50 • Fractured Bumper Stickers

1 Don't follow me.
I'm lost too.

2 I'm not a complete idiot
some parts are missing.

3 My other bumper
sticker is funny.

4 Out of my mind
(back in 5 minutes)

5 4 out of 3 people have
trouble with fractions

6 I may be slow but
I'm ahead of you!

page 51 • Field Trip

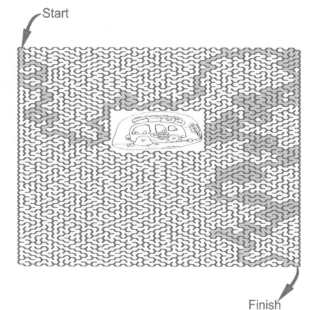

Start

Finish

page 52 • California License Plate

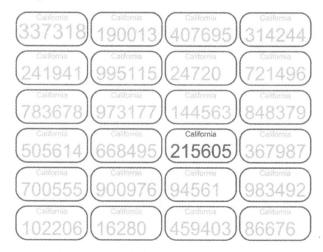

California 337318
California 190013
California 407695
California 314244

California 241941
California 995115
California 24720
California 721496

California 783678
California 973177
California 144563
California 848379

California 505614
California 668495
California 215605
California 367987

California 700555
California 900976
California 94561
California 983492

California 102206
California 16280
California 459403
California 86676

page 53 • Road Map

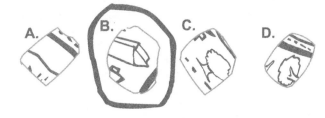

A.   B.   C.   D.

page 54 • Crisscross Country

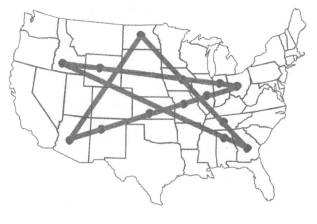

Puzzle Answers

page 54 • Crisscross Country

Live Free or Die — New Hampshire
Great Potatoes. Tasty Destinations. — Idaho
The Evergreen State — Washington
The Islands of Aloha — Hawaii
It's Good Being First — Delaware
Land of Enchantment — New Mexico
Greatest Snow on Earth — Utah
The Heart of Dixie — Alabama
The Grand Canyon State — Arizona
Fields of Opportunity — Iowa

page 55 • Capital Anagrams

THORN LACES
Charleston, West Virginia

TICKET ROLL
Little Rock, Arkansas

DR. EVEN
Denver, Colorado

HALL VINES
Nashville, Tennessee

NO METRO GYM
Montgomery, Alabama

INLAID PIANOS
Indianapolis, Indiana

EAT FANS
Santa Fe, New Mexico

SMART CANOE
Sacramento, California

HIP OXEN
Phoenix, Arizona

page 56 • Mileage

Vince can travel a total of 90 miles (2.5 gallons x 36 miles per gallon). This means that Vince can go up to 45 miles from home and still have enough gas to return. Adding up the mileage, we see that Vince can go to any of these places: **Skateboard Park**
Lake
Mountains
Beach

page 58 • Do You Remember?

1. What animal has its tongue hanging out?
A dog

2. What states are the two license plates from?
Colorado and California

3. Is the tree to the left or right of the bridge in the picture?
Right

4. Is there a stop sign on the page?
No

5. What does the sign shaped like an X say?
RAILROAD CROSSING

6. What is carrying the "For Sale" sign?
An Elephant

7. Does the man's tie have stripes?
No

8. What direction is the pickup truck going on the page, left or right?
Right

9. Is there an ambulance on the page?
Yes

10. What letter is directly above the "For Sale" sign?
Q

page 58 • Road Designer

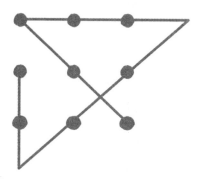

page 59 • Postcards

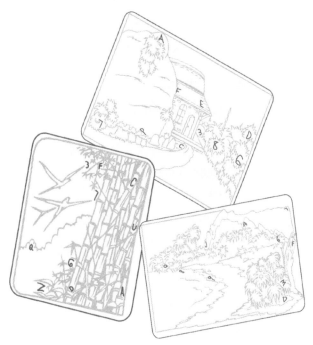

page 60 • Road Riddles

A. Talking informally, especially on the Internet.

C H A T
11 12 13 4

B. A state of mind: happy, sad, angry, etc.

M O O D
10 6 7 1

C. Married to the Queen.

K I N G
8 9 14 15

D. Lincoln lived in a ___ cabin.

L O G
5 2 18

E. A hotel or restaurant.

I N N
16 17 3

1B	2D	3E		4A			
D	O	N	'	T			
5D	**6B**	**7B**	**8C**		**9C**		**10B**
L	O	O	K		I	'	M
11A	**12A**	**13A**	**14C**	**15C**	**16E**	**17E**	**18D**
C	H	A	N	G	I	N	G

page 60 • What Would You call . . .

For each letter, substitute the letter that comes after it in the alphabet.

A PINK CAR NATION

–   – – – –   – – –   – – – – – –

B QJOL DBS OBUJPO

SILVER

– – – – – –

TJMWFS

Puzzle Answers

page 62 • **Rapid Response**

1 It will take the police car six minutes.

3 It will take the ambulance seven and a half minutes.

2 It will take the fire engine seven minutes.

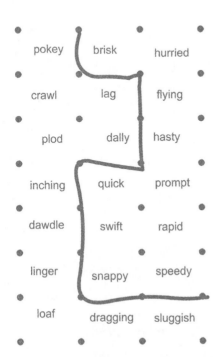

pokey • brisk • hurried

crawl • lag • flying

plod • dally • hasty

inching • quick • prompt

dawdle • swift • rapid

linger • snappy • speedy

loaf • dragging • sluggish

page 63 • **Fire Hose**

page 64 • **Here Spots!**

The number of spots on a dog matches the fire engine number.

Dalmatians were useful in the early days of fire fighting because they were not afraid of the **horses** that pulled the fire engine. This dog would run out in front and clear the streets for the approaching fire engine.

The EVERYTHING KIDS' Cars and Trucks Puzzle and Activity Book

page 65 • Speedy Driver

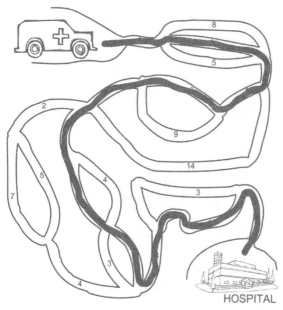

It will take the ambulance 38 minutes to get to the hospital.

page 67 • Clueless Crisis

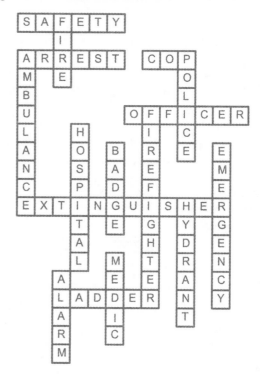

page 66 • Catch a Thief

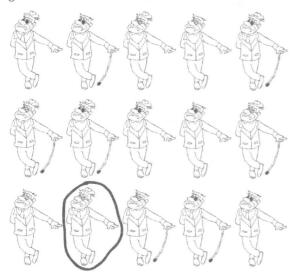

page 68 • Ambulance Amusements

A. Continent

$\underline{A}$ $\underline{F}$ $\underline{R}$ $\underline{I}$ $\underline{C}$ $\underline{A}$
  3   7   5   11 12 1

B. Truck

$\underline{S}$ $\underline{E}$ $\underline{M}$ $\underline{I}$
 13   9   8   4

C. Peas in a

$\underline{P}$ $\underline{O}$ $\underline{D}$
 2   6   10

1A		2C	3A	4B	5A		6C	7A	
A		P	A	I	R		O	F	
8B	9B	10C	11A	12A	13B				
M	E	D	I	C	S				

The surgeon was the boy's mother.

Puzzle Answers

page 69 • Add a Siren

Add a siren to O, rearrange the letters, and get an elder.

S E N I O R

Add a siren to M, rearrange the letters, and get ore extractors.

M I N E R S

Add a siren to D and F, rearrange the letters, and get the keeper, not the weeper.

F I N D E R S

Add a siren to G, rearrange the letters, and get a vocalist.

S I N G E R

Add a siren to D, rearrange the letters, and get people eating.

D I N E R S

page 70 • Safety Rules

This helps put out fires: E X T I N G U I S H E R

Riding these brings more kids to the hospital emergency room than any other sport: B I K E S

Your house should have one of these on every floor to prevent fires: S M O K E   A L A R M

Never put metal in this appliance: M I C R O W A V E

Never touch anything electrical if you are W E T

Always re-latch this to protect young brothers and sisters from danger: S A F E T Y   G A T E

HELMET: the smartest thing you can wear while riding a bike or skateboard.

page 71 • Hardware Burglar Chase

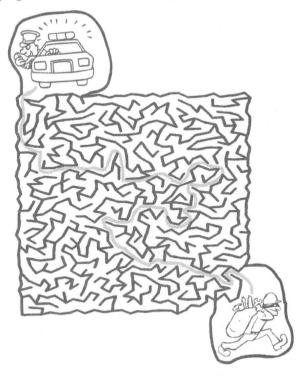

page 72 • Antique Fire Engines

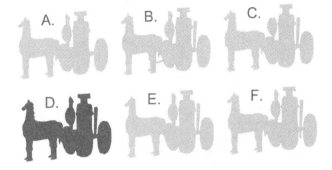

Benjamin Franklin formed the first fire department in America. He also studied electricity by flying a kite in a storm.

page 74 • **Speedy Mart**

1. cookies
2. coffee
3. candy
4. soda
5. gum

Jake bought soda and gum.
Sally bought cookies and candy.
Ronald bought soda, gum, and candy.

page 75 • **Check Your Oil!**

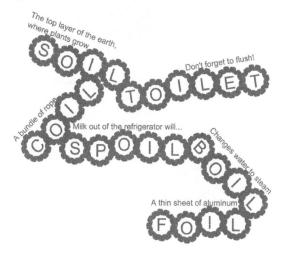

page 76 • **Who Broke it?**

Justin broke the car.

page 76 • **Age?**

Frank is nine years old.

page 77 • **Tire Rotation**

There are 24 ways that four different tires can be put onto four axles.

page 77 • **Fill It Up With What?**

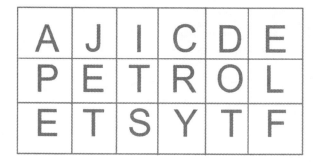

A	J	I	C	D	E
P	E	T	R	O	L
E	T	S	Y	T	F

page 78 • **Doctor Ottoman's Barn**

BATTERY   NUT   PULLEY
ROPE   LADDER

BOLT   WHEEL   GEARS
HORN   HOOK   WRENCH

Puzzle Answers

page 79 • **Doctor Ottoman's Barn**

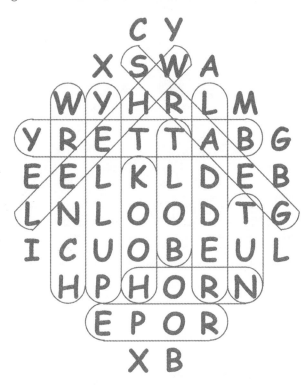

page 80 • **Find Andy's Key**

page 81 • **Ask for Directions**

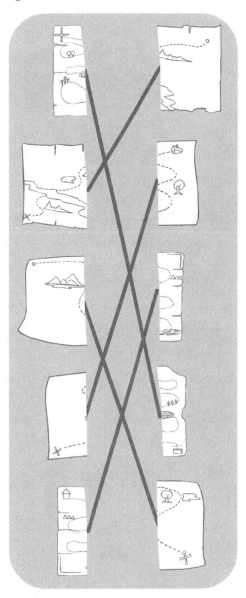

After following the directions, you will be **nine miles east** from the starting point.

The EVERYTHING KIDS' Cars and Trucks Puzzle and Activity Book

page 82 • Tire Balancing Act

page 86 • Mathemagical Roof

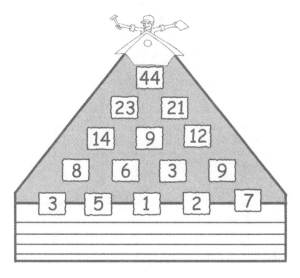

page 83 • Matt's Boxes

2	7	6
9	5	1
4	3	8

2	9	4
7	5	3
6	1	8

4	9	2
3	5	7
8	1	6

4	3	8
9	5	1
2	7	6

6	7	2
1	5	9
8	3	4

6	1	8
7	5	3
2	9	4

page 87 • Tractor Pull

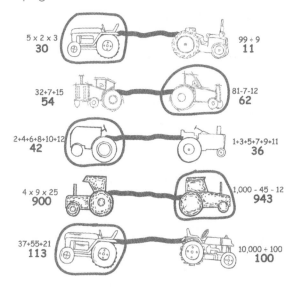

page 84 • Four Wheel Drive

Puzzle Answers

page 88 • **All Mixed Up**

HAMMER
SHOVEL
DRILL
SAW
CLAMP
SCREWDRIVER

page 89 • **Smileys Everywhere**

page 90 • **Give a Lift**

page 92 • **Wireman Wayne**

What kind of car does an electrician drive?

A (V)(O)(L)(T)(S) WAGON

page 93 • **A Site to See**

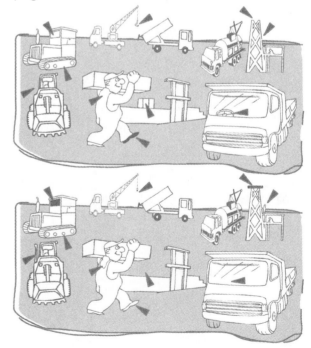

page 94 • Letter Bulldozers

Here are some words found in BULLDOZERS:

bed bell blue blur bold bored boulder bred bud bull bus do doe does doll dose double doze dub due duel dull duo lobe lore lose loser loud lube ode old or orb ore our red rob robe rod role roll rose rosebud rub rude rule sell sled slob slur so sod sold sour sub sue sure us use zero

You may have found others. More words can be made by adding letters to these words.

page 95 • Construction Crossword

page 96 • Gravel Movers

Here is a solution:
1. Fill up the 5 ton truck with gravel.
2. Pour gravel from the 5 ton truck into the 3 ton truck until it is full. The 5 ton truck will have 2 tons of gravel remaining.
3. Empty the 3 ton truck.
4. Pour the 2 tons of gravel from the 5 ton truck into the 3 ton truck.
5. Fill up the 5 ton truck with gravel again.
6. Pour gravel from the 5 ton truck into the 3 ton truck until it is full. Since the 3 ton truck already had 2 tons in it, only 1 ton from the 5 ton truck will be poured.

The 5 ton truck will now have the 4 tons of gravel needed at the construction site.

page 96 • Farmer Joe

Farmer Joe hauls the goose to his barn, then returns to the woods. He hauls the fox to his barn and returns to the woods with the goose. He leaves the goose and hauls the grain to his barn. Farmer Joe returns to the woods and hauls the goose to his barn. Everything has been safely moved to Farmer Joe's barn.

Puzzle Answers

page 98 • nICE Words

page 99 • Favorite Flavors

page 100 • Frosty Riddles

What gets wetter the more it dries?
A towel

Why did the lion eat the tightrope walker?
So he could have a balanced meal

What do you get from a pampered cow?
Spoiled milk

What do you get when you cross a snowman with a vampire?
Frostbite

Where do snowmen keep their money?
In a snow bank

When is a door not a door?
When it is ajar

page 101 • Ice Cream Across America

START

FINISH

page 104 • The Next Ice Cream Bar

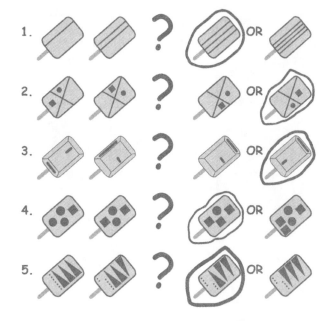

1. ? OR

2. ? OR

3. ? OR

4. ? OR

5. ? OR

page 102 • A Sweet Treat

What is a dull taxi?
DRAB CAB

What do you call a wheat railroad?
GRAIN TRAIN

What is an angry father?
MAD DAD

What is a 50% chuckle?
HALF LAUGH

What is a cheerful father?
HAPPY PAPPY

What is a false serpent?
FAKE SNAKE

What do you call a soggy tent?
DAMP CAMP

What are some very odd coins in your pocket?
STRANGE CHANGE

What is a hat for afternoon slumber?
NAP CAP

What is a doggy kiss?
POOCH SMOOCH

What is a frightening milk provider?
SCARY DAIRY

What is a crazy kid?
WILD CHILD

What are pleasant rodents?
NICE MICE

What do you call a better-looking personal instructor?
CUTER TUTOR

What do you call a tire bargain?
WHEEL DEAL

Puzzle Answers

page 105 • Sharing

Olivia has 7 cents.
Louis has 11 cents.
Paul has 12 cents.
Together they have 30 cents, just enough to buy the ice cream bar.

page 105 • Ice Cream Trivia

Chocolate syrup is the most popular topping for ice cream.

Vanilla is by far the most popular flavor of ice cream.

George Washington was the first U.S. President to eat ice cream. He loved ice cream!

The first hand-cranked ice cream freezer was patented in the year **1848**.

page 106 • Sweet Menu

Each flavor has four possible toppings. There are 6 flavors. So the answer is 6 x 4, or **24** different combinations.

page 106 • For the Very Hungry

5+4+3+2+1=**15** scoops in an ice cream pyramid with five scoops at the base.

page 107 • Exact Change

Here are the coins required for each treat:

18¢ = 10¢ + 5¢ + 1¢ + 1¢ + 1¢ (5 coins)

29¢ = 25¢ + 1¢ + 1¢ + 1¢ + 1¢ (5 coins)

61¢ = 25¢ + 25¢ + 10¢ + 1¢ (4 coins)

63¢ = 25¢ + 25¢ + 10¢ + 1¢ + 1¢ + 1¢ (6 coins)

68¢ = 25¢ + 25¢ + 10¢ + 5¢ + 1¢ + 1¢ + 1¢ (7 coins)

87¢ = 25¢ + 25¢ + 25¢ + 10¢ + 1¢ + 1¢ (6 coins)

95¢ = 25¢ + 25¢ +25¢ + 10¢ + 10¢ (5 coins)

The 61¢ treat can be bought with the fewest number of coins.

The 68¢ treat requires the most number of coins.

page 108 • Candy Please

Jill wants a candy cane.
Frank wants sweet hearts.
Emma wants chocolate.
Erica wants gum.
Carlos wants chocolate.

The Everything®  Series!

Packed with tons of information, activities, and puzzles, the Everything® Kids' books are perennial bestsellers that keep kids active and engaged.

Each book is two-color, 8" x 9¼", and 144 pages.

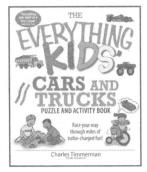

The Everything® Kids' Cars and
Trucks Puzzle and Activity Book
1-59337-703-7, $7.95

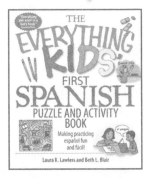

The Everything® Kids' First Spanish
Puzzle and Activity Book
1-59337-717-7, $7.95

The Everything® Kids' Learning
Spanish Book
1-59337-716-9, $7.95

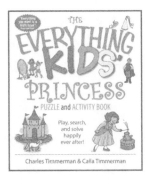

The Everything® Kids'
Princess Puzzle and Activity Book
1-59337-704-5, $7.95

A silly, goofy, and undeniably icky addition to
the Everything® Kids' series . . .

The Everything® Kids'

GROSS
Series

Chock-full of sickening entertainment for hours of disgusting fun.

The Everything® Kids'
Gross Jokes Book
1-59337-448-8, $7.95

The Everything® Kids' Gross
Puzzle & Activity Book
1-59337-447-X, $7.95

The Everything® Kids'
Gross Mazes Book
1-59337-616-2, $7.95

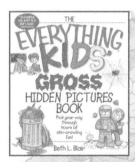

The Everything® Kids' Gross
Hidden Pictures Book
1-59337-615-4, $7.95

Other Everything® Kids' Titles Available

The Everything® Kids' Animal Puzzle & Activity Book
1-59337-305-8

The Everything® Kids' Baseball Book, 4th Ed.
1-59337-614-6

The Everything® Kids' Bible Trivia Book
1-59337-031-8

The Everything® Kids' Bugs Book
1-58062-892-3

The Everything® Kids' Christmas Puzzle & Activity Book
1-58062-965-2

The Everything® Kids' Cookbook
1-58062-658-0

The Everything® Kids' Crazy Puzzles Book
1-59337-361-9

The Everything® Kids' Dinosaurs Book
1-59337-360-0

The Everything® Kids' Halloween Puzzle &
Activity Book
1-58062-959-8

The Everything® Kids' Hidden Pictures Book
1-59337-128-4

The Everything® Kids' Horses Book
1-59337-608-1

The Everything® Kids' Joke Book
1-58062-686-6

The Everything® Kids' Knock Knock Book
1-59337-127-6

The Everything® Kids' Math Puzzles Book
1-58062-773-0

The Everything® Kids' Mazes Book
1-58062-558-4

The Everything® Kids' Money Book
1-58062-685-8

The Everything® Kids' Nature Book
1-58062-684-X

The Everything® Kids' Pirates Puzzle and Activity Book
1-59337-607-3

The Everything® Kids' Puzzle Book
1-58062-687-4

The Everything® Kids' Riddles & Brain Teasers Book
1-59337-036-9

The Everything® Kids' Science Experiments Book
1-58062-557-6

The Everything® Kids' Sharks Book
1-59337-304-X

The Everything® Kids' Soccer Book
1-58062-642-4

The Everything® Kids' Travel Activity Book
1-58062-641-6

All titles are $6.95 or $7.95 unless otherwise noted.

Available wherever books are sold!
To order, call 800-258-0929, or visit us at *www.adamsmedia.com*